COFFEE CAKES

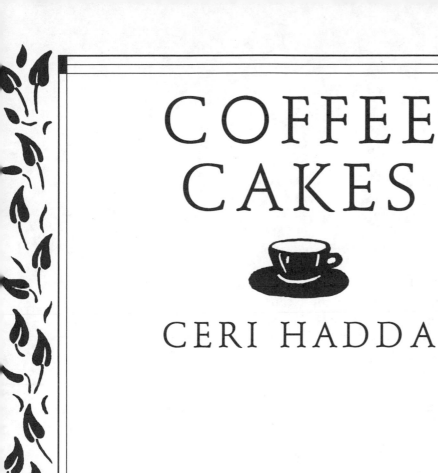

CERI HADDA

SIMON & SCHUSTER

NEW YORK   LONDON   TORONTO   SYDNEY   TOKYO   SINGAPORE

SIMON & SCHUSTER
Simon & Schuster Building
1230 Avenue of the Americas
New York, New York, 10020

Copyright © 1992 by Ceri Hadda

SIMON & SCHUSTER and colophon are registered trade-
marks of Simon & Schuster Inc.
Designed by Barbara Cohen Aronica
Manufactured in the United States of America

10 9 8 7 6 5 4 3 2 1

Library of Congress Cataloging-in-Publication Data

Hadda, Ceri
    Coffee cakes / Ceri Hadda.
        p.   cm.
      1. Coffee cakes. I. Title.
    TX771.H23   1991
      641.8'659—dc20   89-48419
    ISBN 0-671-76109-9   CIP

To Mom, Janet, Kathy, and Allan
for their love, support, and eager palates

ACKNOWLEDGMENTS

To Mary Caldwell, who provided her unerring eye and singular creativity in editing my proposal.

To Jane Dystel for her exacting nature and neverending spirit.

To Toula Polygalaktos and Gail Winston, who seamlessly shared in changing a manuscript into a book.

To Nick Malgieri and Richard Sax, quintessential pros who set the standard.

To Pat Baird, friend and colleague, who generously tested recipes above and beyond the call of duty.

To Anna Teresa Callen, Bill Rice, Lorna Sass, and Lyn Stallworth for their professional guidance, encouragement, and friendship.

To Bill Stites, photographer nonpareil.

To Ann and John Alkire, Robin and Bob Anesi, Eddie Bakhash and Jackie Blank, Susan and Michael Barnes, Steve Bennett, Susan Bosworth, Matt Caputo, Matthew Eichner, Claire Fiala, Kathy George, the Kahl family, Helen and Christian Miles, Lili Ng, Susan Solomon, Jena Wright, and Andy Zerman for their invaluable help in tasting and testing.

And finally, to the men at the Jefferson Market, who make buying groceries a pleasure instead of a chore.

CONTENTS

INTRODUCTION

Which came first, the coffee or the cake? Growing up in a household where my mother baked everything—from crumb-bedecked *streusel kuchen* to deeply flavored marble cake—from scratch, I learned the virtues of simple baking. Since I knew nothing else, I naturally assumed that all baking was as straightforward and satisfying as my mother's.

It was only when I attended restaurant school and encountered the likes of multitiered opera tortes and whipped ganache creams that I realized how complex baking could be. Still, when I went home to my own kitchen, I always hearkened back to those honest cakes of my childhood. And I still do.

The coffee cake is cozy baking at its best. Its very name evokes homey images: good friends sharing confidences over coffee and cake, families gathering for a leisurely weekend breakfast, or perhaps a neighbor welcoming newcomers to the block with a still-warm crumb cake. No highfalutin torte or layered extravaganza, the coffee cake is casual fare meant to be enjoyed in informal settings.

While some coffee cakes are made with yeast, those in the quick category are leavened with baking powder and/or baking soda. This

latter group of coffee cakes reconciles the home baker's desire to prepare a warm, from-scratch product with the perennial need for delicious, fast recipes.

Quick coffee cakes fall somewhere between muffins and cakes in preparation, texture, and flavor. Like muffins, they are usually prepared in one bowl, baked in one pan, and served without further ado. Although often rich with butter, eggs, and sour cream, coffee cakes are less sweet than most standard cakes, since they are typically left unembellished except for a light drift of confectioner's sugar or an occasional glaze.

Quick coffee cakes appeal to both novice and experienced bakers. They are accessible to the fledgling baker because they require little previous knowledge and no specialized bakeware. But even the most seasoned bakers need a varied supply of fast, simple recipes in their repertoire.

CHAPTER 1

BASIC COFFEE CAKE BAKING TECHNIQUES AND INGREDIENTS

Although typically simple to prepare, coffee cakes, like other baked goods, require the right ingredients for best results. Once the ingredients are selected, they must be properly handled.

This chapter provides information on the basic ingredients you'll be using in the recipes that follow. It also covers the rudimentary baking techniques required for best results.

In addition, I've included a little conversion chart for substituting one pan for another.

BASIC INGREDIENTS

Needless to say, a cake is only as good as the ingredients that go into it. Fresh creamery butter, sound, juicy fruits, and pure extracts are just several of the components that add to a cake's final flavor.

Butter. All recipes using butter in this book have been created and tested using *unsalted (or "sweet") butter.* Salted butter is unpredictable, and because of the salt, it may have been lying around the store too long; but if that is what you have, reduce or eliminate the salt called for in the recipe.

Never use whipped or light butter, since their added water and air will adversely affect the cake you make.

Since butter and margarine have the same amount of calories, the only reason to use the latter in baking is to reduce cholesterol and to save a few pennies. Personally, I find the satisfying flavor of butter well worth it, and I'd rather eat a small sliver of a butter cake than a larger one made with margarine.

Butter freezes well, so I buy large quantities on sale and store them in the freezer. Most of the 1-pound packages are already wrapped in plastic, which makes the butter more impervious to picking up off-flavors from the freezer. At 0 degrees Centigrade or lower, the butter keeps well for up to nine months.

Milk. I always use fresh whole milk, never ultrapasteurized or ultrahigh-temperature (UHT)-processed. The latter two methods subject the milk to temperatures that give it a "cooked" flavor undesirable for baking.

Sour Cream and Yogurt. In the preparation of sour cream, heavy cream is pasteurized, then homogenized two times before it is inoculated with bacteria chosen for the acidity and flavor they will impart. Once ripened, the sour cream is aged in the refrigerator for up to two days before it is distributed to be sold.

Yogurt is prepared in a similar way, from whole, low-fat, or nonfat milk. Although yogurt is perceivably more tangy and less creamy than sour cream, I find it can be substituted ounce for ounce for sour cream in any coffee cake recipe. Obviously, the added fat associated with sour cream will make a cake extra tender and moist. Nonetheless, the presence of other ingredients such as butter and eggs usually benefits the cake's texture, too.

Keep both sour cream and yogurt refrigerated until just before you will be using them. Never freeze either of them, since they separate easily.

Heavy or Whipping Cream. Although heavy or whipping cream, which contains not less than 36 percent milk fat, occasionally plays

a part in a coffee cake batter, it is more often used in fillings and glazes.

Always buy cream from a reliable source where you know it has been kept under constant refrigeration. Once you get it home, immediately place it in the refrigerator, where it should keep for at least a week. Do not freeze cream, since its texture will be altered.

Whenever possible, I use fresh, rather than ultrapasteurized, cream, although I don't notice as marked a difference here as I do between fresh and UHT milk.

Buttermilk. I often rely on buttermilk to add a tender, tangy quality to coffee cakes. Although its rich-sounding moniker refers to its original role as a by-product of butter making, today's commercially available buttermilk has no butter in it at all; in fact, its fat profile is more similar to that of skim milk. In a process similar to the one for preparing yogurt and sour cream, buttermilk is fermented from skim or low-fat milk, blended with nonfat dry milk for added thickness, and combined with bacterial cultures. The milk, often salted, is pasteurized to destroy harmful bacteria before it is inoculated with the appropriate cultures. During an incubation period of twelve to twenty-four hours, the milk's lactose turns to lactic acid, creating the characteristic tang associated with buttermilk.

Buttermilk keeps in the refrigerator for up to two weeks. If you're an infrequent user of buttermilk, the powdered variety, now widely available, is a perfect substitution. Or, add a teaspoon or two of lemon juice or vinegar to a cup of milk, and let it stand until it curdles and sours.

Eggs. All recipes in this book have been created and tested using *extra-large eggs.* If you're substituting eggs of a different size, a handy rule of thumb is one large egg equals 2 ounces (¼ cup); one extra-large egg equals 2¼ ounces, and one jumbo egg equals 2½ ounces.

Buy clean, uncracked grade A or AA eggs from refrigerated cases. Once you get home, refrigerate the eggs immediately and keep them refrigerated until you'll be using them. Do not store eggs in the egg shelf of your refrigerator door; they will be subject to repeated temperature fluctuations and breakage. Instead, keep the eggs in the carton you bought them in, which also inhibits the absorption of refrigerator odors. Turn them large-end-up to keep the yolks centered.

• Store whole eggs in the refrigerator for up to four or five weeks beyond the pack date. Always keep eggs refrigerated until just before you'll be using them (if a recipe calls for room-temperature eggs, thirty minutes out of the refrigerator should suffice); room-temperature eggs age seven times more quickly than those kept under refrigeration.

• Store egg whites in a tightly closed container in the refrigerator for up to four days.

• Store unbroken egg yolks in water to cover in a tightly closed container in the refrigerator. Use within a day or two.

• Never freeze whole eggs in their shells.

• To freeze egg yolks, stir ⅛ teaspoon salt or 1½ teaspoons sugar or corn syrup into every four yolks, noting which you've added on a label.

- To freeze whole eggs, beat together just until blended before pouring into the freezer container.

- To freeze egg whites, no special treatment is needed, though for easier measuring, the whites can be frozen in ice cube trays, unmolded, and stored in plastic freezer bags.

- To thaw frozen eggs, whites, or yolks, refrigerate overnight or place the closed container under running cold water. Use the yolks or whole eggs at once. Let the egg whites sit at room temperature for about 30 minutes if you'll be whipping them.

Cream Cheese. Whenever possible, I use natural cream cheese free of gums and other additives; not surprisingly, it has a lighter, less "gummy" texture. Whipped cream cheese, aerated to make it fluffy, is not suitable for recipes in this book.

Only buy as much cream cheese as you'll be using for a particular recipe, since it does not keep well. Never freeze cream cheese.

Oil. For baking, I use corn oil or a tasteless blend. Some bakers like the more pronounced flavor of a light olive oil; except in the case of special Italian recipes, I can't say that I feel the same way.

Although there are no recipes in this book using walnut, almond, or hazelnut oils, they can be used in combination with vegetable oil to add their nutty essence.

Sugar. I always have granulated, light and dark brown, and confectioner's sugar on hand.

Since I bake frequently, and since granulated sugar lasts indefinitely, I buy 5-pound bags and transfer the sugar to a large glass jar once I've opened the bag. Before making your purchase, check to see that there are few lumps in the sugar by pressing the bag; they'll be a nuisance come baking time.

Brown sugar adds a deep, molasses flavor as well as moisture to batters. Most of the recipes in this book call for one or the other, but you can interchange them or use a combination. Before you buy either sugar, gently squeeze the package to ensure that the sugar is moist. Once you've opened a package, wrap the remainder in a second plastic bag. Rock-hard brown sugar can be softened with a brief stint in a 300-degree oven, but the sugar must be used at once or it will reharden. I've also grated the sugar against a hand grater, although it will not provide the same moist results.

Confectioner's powdered (10×) sugar is used as a base for glazes and frostings, as well as dusted onto cakes that need no more elaborate treatment than that. Since it tends to form lumps, sift before measuring and using it.

Honey and Maple Syrup. For general baking, I use an all-purpose blend of honey, one that is mild enough to harmonize with the other ingredients. To minimize crystallization, it should be stored in an airtight container in a cool place, and in the refrigerator for long-term storage. If it *does* crystallize, place the jar of honey in a saucepan of hot water and heat until the crystals have liquefied.

For baking, I use an amber-colored grade A maple syrup that is pure but not so strong that it will overpower the other ingredients in my recipe. I always keep opened containers of maple syrup in the refrigerator, since they tend to go moldy if they're left out too long.

Flour, All-Purpose. For years, I used all-purpose unbleached flour in all of my baking except for the most delicate of cakes. Lately, however, I've noticed that a lot of unbleached flour is very lumpy. So, I've gone back to *bleached all-purpose flour*, and that is what I used for all of the recipes in this book.

Flour, Whole-Wheat. Whole-wheat flour adds a nutty flavor and nice "chew" to some coffee cakes. I like buying stone-ground whole-wheat flour because of its pronounced flavor and texture. If it's hot, or if I won't be using up the flour for a while, I refrigerate it to avoid rancidity.

Leaveners. Baking soda and baking powder are essential ingredients in quick coffee cakes. Store them in a cool, dry place. Since they should be of optimum freshness for best leavening action, I replace them often. All recipes in this book use double-acting baking powder.

Chocolate and Cocoa. Since I'm a confirmed chocolate lover, I always have a supply of unsweetened and semisweet chocolate on hand, as well as a tin of good-quality unsweetened cocoa powder.

Unsweetened chocolate is available in 1-ounce squares. For most of my semisweet chocolate needs, I buy 3-ounce bars of dark Swiss chocolate. If a recipe calls for it, I also use good-quality semisweet chocolate pieces; the mini-size are especially convenient for baking because they easily permeate the batter.

Never buy presweetened cocoa powder, only the unsweetened variety. If it is lumpy, sift it before measuring. For recipes in this book, I've used regular cocoa, not the milder, somewhat darker,

"Dutched" or alkalized variety. (In a pinch, 3 tablespoons of un-sweetened cocoa and 1 tablespoon of solid vegetable shortening can be used in place of a 1-ounce square of unsweetened chocolate.)

All chocolate keeps almost indefinitely if it's stored in a cool, dark place. Don't be alarmed if the chocolate turns white; that's just the cocoa butter coming to the surface in a "bloom." The chocolate is still perfectly usable.

The microwave is an ideal aid in melting chocolate for recipes, whether they are traditionally baked or finished in the microwave.

Cornmeal. I've always loved adding ½ cup or so of cornmeal to a batter; it adds a pleasant grittiness to a cake. Whenever possible, I buy stone-ground cornmeal, because it seems to have a more pro-nounced flavor.

Cornstarch. Cornstarch is used in some of the cakes in this book. It adds a silken tenderness.

Salt. Although I like cooking with coarse (kosher) salt, I find regular salt is preferable for baking, since it dissolves more readily.

Nuts. Just-cracked nuts are usually the freshest, but since I rarely have the time to crack my own, nuts in a can or bag from a store with a high turnover suit me just fine. Freeze what you won't use quickly, in tightly closed bags or containers, to avoid rancidity.

Extracts, Flavorings, and Spices. Extracts, flavorings, and spices are used in such small quantities, yet without them, most coffee cakes would taste dull and lackluster. That's why it makes good sense to

buy only the finest, purest products available. Never, for example, expect artificial vanilla extract to add the alluring perfume of pure vanilla.

With the exception of vanilla and cinnamon, which I find myself using almost every time I bake, I buy flavorings in quantities that I'll be able to use up within a few months. That way, they'll be at their most potent and flavorful when I need them.

Instant espresso coffee powder is a handy flavoring, too. Just a little bit dissolved in hot water enhances chocolate batters and glazes, for example.

Store all flavorings in tightly covered containers in a cool, dark place.

Fresh Fruit. Coffee cakes are the perfect repositories for an overabundance of fruit in season. But while it's fine to use slightly overripe fruit, avoid damaged fruit that is not sound. This will only hasten the spoilage of the cake itself.

TECHNIQUES

Sifting. Sifting dry ingredients through a flour sifter or fine sieve eliminates lumps and ensures an even distribution of leaveners and spices. In most of the recipes in this book, I've listed instructions for sifting. To be perfectly candid, if the flour I'm using seems relatively lump-free, I often vigorously and thoroughly stir together the dry ingredients in a small bowl, using a wire whip instead of sifting.

Creaming. Creaming is the term used to describe beating butter on its own or with sugar, until it becomes soft and light. Room-temperature butter is easier to cream than ice-cold butter. Cream butter until it softens and begins to aerate, scraping the sides of the bowl often with a rubber spatula. When sugar is added to the butter as it is creamed, the butter whitens and becomes even lighter in texture.

Chopping Nuts. To chop nuts by hand, place the nuts, a handful at a time, on a clean, dry chopping board. With a heavy chef's knife, cut the nuts into chunks, then continue chopping until the pieces are the size you wish. With a food processor, nuts can be chopped using on-and-off pulses. Avoid overprocessing, or the nuts will form a paste. One way to minimize this is to add a portion of the sugar called for in the recipe to the nuts in the processor.

Toasting Nuts. Toasting nuts enhances their flavor and adds crunch. Place the nuts in a single layer in a roasting pan. Bake at 350 degrees, stirring often, until the nuts are evenly golden. Watch for burning; the nuts continue to cook from residual heat even when they're removed from the oven.

Blanching Nuts. In the case of hazelnuts, the above toasting method can be taken one step further. Bake the nuts until the skins start to crack and separate from the nuts. Transfer to a tea towel, cover with the towel, and rub vigorously to dislodge as much of the skins as possible. Do not worry if some remain.

For almonds and pistachios, pour boiling water over the nuts in a heatproof bowl; let stand a few minutes, then drain. Working

quickly, press the nuts out of their skins; the skins should be loose enough so that the nuts pop out of them.

PAN SUBSTITUTION

Sometimes a different-size pan can be used instead of the size called for in a recipe. Baking temperatures and times will usually need to be altered.

To measure pan volumes, I fill the pan with a known quantity of water. Then I mark the volume of the pan on the bottom of the pan with nail polish, so I can keep track of the volume without having to measure it each time.

Only fill a cake pan two-thirds full with batter, to allow for rising in the oven.

To adapt recipes to pans of varied sizes, use those with the same batter yield, listed below.

ROUND PANS

6-inch pan holds 1¼ cups batter

8-inch pan holds 2¼ cups batter

9-inch pan holds 2½ cups batter

10-inch pan holds 3⅔ cups batter

11-inch pan holds 4¼ cups batter

12-inch pan holds 5¾ cups batter

SQUARE PANS

8-inch pan holds 3½ cups batter

10-inch pan holds 6 cups batter

12-inch pan holds 9 cups batter

TUBE PANS

9-inch pan holds 5 cups batter

10-inch angel cake tube pan holds 10 cups batter

10-inch fluted tube pan holds 8 cups batter

12-inch angel cake tube pan holds 16 cups batter

12-inch fluted tube pan holds 12 cups batter

OTHERS

Batter for one 9 by 13 by 2-inch pan fills three 8 by 1½-inch round pans, two 9 by 9 by 2-inch pans, two 9 by 1½-inch round pans, or two 8 by 8 by 2-inch pans

Batter for one 9 by 5 by 3-inch loaf pan fills one 9 by 9 by 2-inch pan

Batter for two 9 by 5 by 3-inch loaf pans fills one 10-inch angel cake tube pan

Batter for one 8 by 4 by 3-inch loaf pan fills one 8 by 8 by 2-inch pan

Batter for one 9-inch angel cake tube pan fills one 10-inch fluted tube pan

CHAPTER 2

CRUMB CAKES

Raspberry Cream Cheese Crumb Cake

Double Chocolate Babka

Little Cinnamon Crumb Cakes

Crumb Cake for a Crowd

Chocolate Peanut Butter Crunch Cake

Snipdoodle

Buttermilk Spice Crumb Cake

Dimple-Top Crumb Cake

Old-Fashioned Butter Crumb Cake

Breakfast Special Cake

Butterscotch Pecan Crumb Cake

Plum Crunch Cake

Blueberry Buckle

Gingersnap Crumb Cake

Pie Plate Coffee Cake

There's something about crumbs that sends hearts aflutter! Perhaps the most popular of all coffee cakes, the crumb cake combines soft, moist cake with a mantle of crunch. Some preparations, such as the Butterscotch Pecan Crumb Cake (page 40), are one-bowl affairs; the crumbs are mixed together, a portion is removed for the topping, and the remaining ingredients are added to make the batter. Others pair a butter- or oil-enriched batter with a separately mixed topping. Crumb cakes run the gamut from simple, old-fashioned butter crumb cakes to layered babkas filled with chocolate or cheese and preserves. Most should be eaten warm from the oven or soon after that, to preserve the balance between the tender batter and the crisp topping.

RASPBERRY CREAM CHEESE CRUMB CAKE

In this cake, a berry-studded cream cheese filling comes between the batter and the crumb topping. Instead of raspberries, you can use blackberries, blueberries, or even stewed blackcurrants or loganberries.

MAKES ONE 9-INCH CAKE, 8 SERVINGS

The Cheese Filling
1 package (8 ounces) natural cream cheese, at room temperature
½ cup sugar
¼ teaspoon grated lemon zest
1 tablespoon lemon juice
1 egg yolk
1 tablespoon all-purpose flour
1 teaspoon kirsch or raspberry eau-de-vie, optional

The Crumbs
6 tablespoons unsalted butter, at room temperature
1 cup all-purpose flour
⅓ cup sugar

continued on next page

Raspberry Cream Cheese Crumb Cake (*cont.*)

The Cake
1 stick plus 2 tablespoons (5 ounces) unsalted butter, at room tem-
    perature
¾ cup sugar
2 eggs
1 teaspoon pure vanilla extract
1¼ cups all-purpose flour
½ teaspoon baking powder
¼ teaspoon salt
⅓ cup milk

½ pint raspberries, rinsed carefully and well drained

1. Preheat the oven to 350 degrees. Butter the bottom and sides of a
   9-inch springform pan and set aside.

2. To make the cheese filling beat the cream cheese in a medium
   bowl with a large spoon until it is creamy. Beat in the sugar,
   lemon zest, lemon juice, egg yolk, flour, and kirsch or eau-de-vie.
   Continue beating until the mixture is very smooth, then set aside.

3. To make the crumbs combine the butter, flour, and sugar in a small bowl with a spoon or your fingers until the mixture forms big crumbs, then set aside.

4. To make the cake cream the butter in a large bowl; gradually add the sugar and continue beating until the mixture is light and fluffy. Beat in the eggs, one at a time, then the vanilla.

5. In a small bowl stir together the flour, baking powder, and salt, then add alternately with the milk to the butter mixture, mixing just until blended.

6. Spread the batter in the springform pan, building up the sides slightly. Working to within ½ inch of the edge of the pan, scatter half of the raspberries over the batter, spoon the cheese mixture evenly over the berries, then top with the remaining berries. Scatter the crumbs all over the top, pressing them in gently so they adhere to the batter.

7. Bake until the cake and the crumbs are golden, 1 hour 10 minutes to 1 hour 20 minutes. Cool the cake in the pan on a wire rack.

DOUBLE CHOCOLATE BABKA

Here a chocolate-nut crumb mixture swirls within an intense cocoa batter. Although I usually use Swiss chocolate bars to make the crumbs, semisweet chocolate pieces work well, too.

MAKES ONE 10-INCH TUBE CAKE

The Crumbs
2 bars (3 ounces each) semisweet chocolate, finely chopped, *or* 1
   cup semisweet chocolate pieces
1 cup finely chopped pecans
¼ cup sugar
1 teaspoon ground cinnamon

The Cake
2 cups all-purpose flour
⅓ cup cocoa powder
1½ teaspoons baking powder
¾ teaspoon baking soda
1 teaspoon cinnamon
½ teaspoon salt
1 cup (2 sticks) unsalted butter, softened
1¼ cups sugar
1 teaspoon pure vanilla extract
3 eggs
1 cup sour cream

1. Preheat the oven to 350 degrees. Butter a 10-inch tube pan and set aside.

2. To make the crumbs combine the chocolate, pecans, sugar, and cinnamon in a small bowl and set aside.

3. To make the cake sift together the flour, cocoa powder, baking powder, baking soda, cinnamon, and salt onto a sheet of waxed paper, then set aside.

4. In a medium bowl, beat the butter and sugar with an electric mixer on high speed until light and fluffy. Change the mixer speed to medium and beat in the vanilla, then the eggs, one at a time.

5. Change the mixer speed to low. Alternately beat in the flour mixture and sour cream, beginning and ending with the flour mixture and beating only until blended.

6. Spread half of the batter in the bottom of the prepared pan. Sprinkle with half of the crumb mixture. Top with the remaining batter and crumb mixture, pressing the crumbs in lightly so they adhere to the batter. Quickly but gently cut through the batter and crumbs in an up-and-down motion with a knife. Lightly rap the pan once against a hard surface, to settle the ingredients.

7. Bake for 40 minutes, then cover the top with aluminum foil. Continue baking until a skewer inserted halfway between the side of the pan and the tube comes out clean, about 20 minutes longer.

8. Cool the cake in the pan on a wire rack for 30 minutes. Carefully loosen the cake from around the sides of the pan and of the tube. Invert onto the rack, turn right-side-up, and cool completely.

LITTLE CINNAMON CRUMB CAKES

There's something about having a little cake all to yourself, especially when it's overloaded with buttery crumbs. For apple crumb cakes, quarter, pare, core, and thinly slice a tart green apple. Tuck apple slices into the batter before sprinkling with the crumbs.

MAKES 12 MUFFIN-SIZED CAKES

The Crumbs
½ cup (1 stick) unsalted butter, softened
1 cup all-purpose flour
⅔ cup sugar
2 teaspoons ground cinnamon

The Batter
2¼ cups all-purpose flour
1 cup sugar
1 tablespoon baking powder
¼ teaspoon salt
¾ cup vegetable oil
⅓ cup milk
3 eggs
1 teaspoon pure vanilla extract

1. Preheat the oven to 350 degrees. Butter 12 muffin pans and set aside.

2. To make the crumbs work the butter, flour, sugar, and cinnamon in a small bowl with your fingers until the mixture forms crumbs; set aside.

3. To make the batter sift the flour, sugar, baking powder, and salt into a medium bowl. Add the oil, milk, eggs, and vanilla and beat vigorously with a heavy spoon just until the batter is blended. Do not overbeat.

4. Divide the batter between the prepared muffin pans. Scatter the crumbs over the tops, pressing them in gently.

5. Bake until the tops are golden and springy to the touch and the crumbs are crisp, about 40 minutes. Cool in the pans on a wire rack for 5 minutes. If the cakes have overflowed a bit, cut them apart with a sharp knife. Carefully unmold and serve warm or at room temperature.

CRUMB CAKE FOR A CROWD

This is an adaptation of a recipe that I clipped from the New York Daily News. *Generously crowned with a spicy topping, it's for those individuals who prefer the crumbs to the cake.*

MAKES ONE 9 BY 13-INCH CAKE, 12 SERVINGS

The Crumbs
1⅛ cups (2¼ sticks) unsalted butter, softened
¾ cup firmly packed light brown sugar
½ cup granulated sugar
2 teaspoons ground cinnamon
¼ teaspoon grated or ground nutmeg, optional
3 cups all-purpose flour

The Cake
2 cups all-purpose flour
¾ cup granulated sugar
1 teaspoon salt
1 teaspoon baking powder
2 eggs
1 cup milk
⅓ cup vegetable oil
1½ teaspoons pure vanilla extract

10 × confectioner's sugar, for dusting

1. Preheat the oven to 375 degrees. Butter a 9 by 13-inch baking pan and set aside.

2. To make the crumbs combine the butter, sugars, cinnamon, and nutmeg in a large bowl with a large spoon. Stir in the flour, mixing first with the spoon, then with your fingers, to form big crumbs; set aside.

3. To make the cake combine the flour, sugar, salt, and baking powder in another large bowl. In a small bowl, whisk together the eggs, milk, oil, and vanilla and add to the dry ingredients. Mix just until blended.

4. Spread the batter in the prepared pan; it will be thin. Scatter the crumbs in an even layer over the batter, pressing them in gently.

5. Bake until the crumbs are crisp and the batter is springy when gently pressed with a fingertip, about 45 minutes. Serve warm, topping with a dusting of confectioner's sugar, if desired.

CHOCOLATE PEANUT BUTTER CRUNCH CAKE

Officially affianced since the creation of peanut butter cups, chocolate and peanut butter are a classic pair. The batter for this cake is streaked with molten peanut butter and chocolate before it's sprinkled with the crumbs. For me, there's nothing like milk as an accompaniment.

MAKES ONE 8-INCH CAKE

The Chocolate Peanut Butter Swirl
1 cup semisweet chocolate pieces
¼ cup peanut butter

The Crumbs and Cake
1½ cups all-purpose flour
1 cup firmly packed light brown sugar
½ cup (1 stick) unsalted butter
½ cup natural peanut butter
2 eggs
½ cup milk
1 teaspoon pure vanilla extract
½ teaspoon baking powder
½ teaspoon baking soda

1. Preheat the oven to 350 degrees. Butter an 8-inch square baking pan and set aside.

2. To make the chocolate peanut butter swirl melt the chocolate pieces and peanut butter in a small saucepan over low heat, stirring often until smooth. Remove from the heat; let cool while preparing the crumbs and batter.

3. To make the crumbs combine the flour, brown sugar, butter, and peanut butter in a large bowl until the mixture forms crumbs. Remove ¾ cup (tightly packed) of the mixture and set aside.

4. To make the cake add the eggs to the remaining crumbs in the bowl, then the milk, vanilla, baking powder, and baking soda. Beat with an electric mixer on medium speed for 1 to 2 minutes, or until the batter is smooth.

5. Spread half of the batter in the prepared pan; gently streak half of the chocolate peanut butter mixture over the top. Repeat with the remaining batter and chocolate peanut butter mixture. Scatter the reserved crumbs over the top, pressing them in gently so they adhere to the batter.

6. Bake until the crumbs and top of the cake are firm and a skewer inserted in the center comes out clean, about 50 minutes. Cover the pan loosely with aluminum foil if the cake is getting too dark during baking.

SNIPDOODLE

Lyn Stallworth prepares this feather-light easily assembled Pennsylvania Dutch cake whenever she makes a big Sunday breakfast. "It's something you can shove in the oven while you prepare everything else." While not technically a crumb cake, the homey appeal, crumbly fragility, and hint of spice puts it closer to this category than to any other. Besides its ease of preparation, I love the fact that it requires no special ingredients.

MAKES ONE 8-INCH SQUARE CAKE, 8 SERVINGS

The Cake
1¾ cups all-purpose flour
2 teaspoons baking powder
¼ teaspoon salt
½ cup vegetable shortening
2 tablespoons unsalted butter
¾ cup sugar
1 egg
¾ cup milk

The Cinnamon Sugar
2 or 3 tablespoons sugar
¼ to ½ teaspoon ground cinnamon

1. Preheat the oven to 375 degrees and position the oven rack in the middle of the oven. Butter an 8-inch square baking pan and dust with flour. Set the pan aside. (*Note:* Lyn uses a glass baking pan and bakes the cake at 350 degrees.)

2. To make the cake sift together the flour, baking powder, and salt onto a sheet of waxed paper and set aside.

3. In a large mixing bowl, beat the shortening, butter, and sugar with an electric mixer on high speed until light and fluffy. Beat in the egg.

4. Alternately beat in the dry ingredients with milk, beginning and ending with the dry ingredients. The batter should be smooth, but be careful not to overbeat. Pour the batter into the prepared pan; smooth the top with a spatula.

5. Bake until the cake shrinks slightly away from the sides of the pan and is firm to the touch, about 45 minutes. Place on a wire rack to cool.

6. To make the cinnamon sugar combine the sugar and cinnamon. Sprinkle over the top of the cake and cut into 2-inch squares. Serve warm or at room temperature.

BUTTERMILK SPICE CRUMB CAKE

Buttermilk never fails to impart a particularly moist, tender texture to cakes. This cake is generously topped with spicy crumbs.

MAKES ONE 9 BY 13-INCH CAKE, 12 TO 16 SERVINGS

The Crumbs
½ cup (1 stick) unsalted butter
½ cup granulated sugar
½ cup firmly packed light brown sugar
1½ cups all-purpose flour
1½ teaspoons ground cinnamon
¼ teaspoon ground or grated nutmeg
¼ teaspoon ground cloves

The Cake
2¼ cups all-purpose flour
1½ teaspoons ground cinnamon
½ teaspoon ground ginger
¼ teaspoon ground or grated nutmeg
¼ teaspoon ground cloves
1 teaspoon baking powder
1 teaspoon baking soda
½ teaspoon salt

½ cup (1 stick) unsalted butter, at room temperature
¾ cup firmly packed light brown sugar
½ cup granulated sugar
3 eggs
1¼ cups buttermilk blended with 1 teaspoon pure vanilla extract

10× confectioner's sugar, for dusting

1. Preheat the oven to 350 degrees. Butter a 9 by 13-inch pan and set aside.

2. To make the crumbs combine all of the ingredients in a medium bowl with a spoon or your fingers until the mixture forms coarse crumbs; set aside.

3. To make the cake sift together the flour, cinnamon, ginger, nutmeg, cloves, baking powder, baking soda, and salt onto a sheet of waxed paper; set aside.

4. In a large bowl, beat the butter with an electric mixer on high speed until light and fluffy. Gradually beat in the sugars, beating until very light. Change the mixer speed to medium and beat in the eggs, one at a time, beating well after each addition.

5. Change the mixer speed to low and alternately beat in the flour mixture and buttermilk, beginning and ending with the flour mixture and beating just until blended. Spread the batter in the prepared pan. Scatter the crumbs over the top, pressing them lightly into the batter.

continued on next page

Buttermilk Spice Crumb Cake (*cont.*)

6. Bake until the top of the cake is firm, the crumbs are crisp, and a
   skewer inserted in the cake comes out clean, 40 to 45 minutes.
   Cool in the pan on a wire rack. Dust with the confectioner's sugar
   before serving, if desired.

DIMPLE-TOP CRUMB CAKE

*Like Crumb Cake for a Crowd, this quick-to-mix cake uses oil for the batter and
butter for the topping. As it bakes, the butter forms dimples, much like those that
top a Moravian coffee cake.*

MAKES ONE 8-INCH CAKE, 4 TO 5 SERVINGS

1½ cups all-purpose flour
¾ cup sugar
2 teaspoons baking powder
⅛ teaspoon salt
½ cup vegetable oil
¼ cup milk
2 eggs
2 teaspoons pure vanilla extract
½ cup firmly packed light brown sugar
1 teaspoon ground cinnamon
3 tablespoons unsalted butter

1. Preheat the oven to 350 degrees and set aside an 8-inch baking pan.

2. In a large bowl, combine the flour, sugar, baking powder, and salt.

3. In a medium bowl, stir together the oil, milk, eggs, and vanilla, just until blended. Add to the dry ingredients and mix with a large spoon just until blended. Spread the batter in the ungreased pan.

4. Scatter the brown sugar, then the cinnamon, over the batter. Cut the butter into bits and scatter over the top of the cake.

5. Bake until a skewer inserted in the center of the cake comes out clean and the cake shrinks from the sides of the pan, about 40 minutes. Cool in the pan on a wire rack. Cut into squares and serve warm or at room temperature.

OLD-FASHIONED BUTTER CRUMB CAKE

Simple and satisfying. Because it's a bit sweet, this cake almost requires a cup of coffee as an accompaniment.

MAKES ONE 9-INCH CAKE, 9 TO 12 SERVINGS

The Crumbs
¼ cup (½ stick) unsalted butter, softened
¾ cup all-purpose flour
¼ cup sugar
Few drops pure vanilla extract
¼ teaspoon ground cinnamon

The Cake
1¼ cups all-purpose flour
1 teaspoon baking powder
¼ teaspoon salt
½ cup (1 stick) unsalted butter, softened
¾ cup sugar
2 eggs
⅓ cup milk
1 teaspoon pure vanilla extract

1. Preheat the oven to 350 degrees. Butter a 9-inch square baking pan and set aside.

2. To make the crumbs combine the butter, flour, sugar, vanilla, and cinnamon in a small bowl until the mixture is well blended and forms crumbs; set aside.

3. To make the cake sift together the flour, baking powder, and salt onto a sheet of waxed paper and set aside. In a medium bowl, beat the butter with an electric mixer on high speed until very light. Slowly beat in the sugar and continue beating until fluffy, about 3 minutes.

4. Change the mixer speed to medium. Beat in the eggs, one at a time, beating well after each addition. Change the mixer speed to low. Alternately beat in the sifted dry ingredients and the milk and vanilla, beginning and ending with the dry ingredients and beating only until blended.

5. Spread the batter in the prepared pan, smoothing the top. Scatter the crumbs over the top, pressing them in lightly.

6. Bake until the cake is golden brown and the crumbs are golden and crisp, about 45 minutes. Cool the cake in the pan on a wire rack. Serve warm or at room temperature. Leftover pieces of the cake warm up nicely the next day.

Variations. For Browned Butter Crumb Cake, melt the butter for the crumbs in a small saucepan over moderate heat. Continue cooking,

continued on next page

Old-Fashioned Butter Crumb Cake (*cont.*)
stirring occasionally, until the butter turns golden brown. Be careful that the butter does not burn. Let the butter cool to room temperature, then mix with the remaining crumb ingredients.

For Roasted Hazelnut Crumb Cake, add ½ cup hazelnuts, toasted, skinned, and finely chopped to the crumb mixture.

For Fruit Crumb Cake, top the batter with a layer of sliced apples, blueberries, and/or raspberries or bananas before sprinkling with the crumbs.

BREAKFAST SPECIAL CAKE

Everything's in here except the toast and bacon! This is a double time saver: The crumbs and batter are made in one bowl and the recipe makes two tender cakes, one for now, the other for reheating the next day or for freezing.

MAKES TWO 8- OR 9-INCH CAKES

3 cups all-purpose flour
1 cup firmly packed light brown sugar
¾ cup honey
1 tablespoon ground cinnamon
½ teaspoon salt
¾ cup (1½ sticks) unsalted butter, softened
1 cup walnuts, chopped
2 cups corn, wheat, and/or rice flake cereal
2 teaspoons baking powder

½ teaspoon baking soda
2 eggs
½ cup milk
½ cup orange or apple juice
½ cup extrastrong coffee
1 teaspoon pure vanilla extract

1. Preheat the oven to 350 degrees. Butter 2 8- or 9-inch baking pans and set aside.

2. In a large bowl, combine the flour, brown sugar, honey, cinnamon, and salt with your fingers until blended. Mix in the butter; the mixture will be soft.

3. Remove 1 cup of the mixture to a small bowl; mix in the nuts and cereal and set aside.

4. Add the baking powder and baking soda to the remaining crumbs in the large bowl. Beat in the eggs, then the milk, juice, coffee, and vanilla.

5. Divide the batter between the 2 pans; top each with equal portions of the crumb mixture.

6. Bake until the cakes shrink from the sides of the pans and a skewer inserted in the centers comes out clean, 50 to 55 minutes. The cakes will be soft and extra springy because of the honey in the batter. For crisp toppings, let the cakes cool completely in the pans on a wire rack. For soft toppings, loosely cover the cakes with aluminum foil after cooling for 15 or 20 minutes.

BUTTERSCOTCH PECAN CRUMB CAKE

Within the category of crumb cakes are those where the crumb mixture is made first, a small amount is removed for topping the cake, and leaveners and liquid are added to the remainder to make the batter. The recipe can be doubled and baked in two 8-inch pans or in one 9 by 13-inch pan.

MAKES ONE 8- OR 9-INCH CAKE

1¼ cups all-purpose flour
1 cup firmly packed light or dark brown sugar
¼ teaspoon salt
⅓ cup (generous 5 tablespoons) butter, softened
1 cup chopped pecans
1 teaspoon baking powder
¼ teaspoon baking soda
½ cup buttermilk
2 teaspoons pure vanilla extract
1 egg, beaten well

1. Preheat the oven to 350 degrees. Butter an 8- or 9-inch round or square baking pan; dust with flour, tapping out the excess, and set aside.

2. Into a medium bowl, sift together the flour, sugar, and salt. Add the butter. With a pastry blender, 2 knives, or your fingers, work the mixture to form fine crumbs. Remove ½ cup of the crumbs; add the pecans and set aside.

3. To the crumbs remaining in the bowl, add the baking powder and baking soda, then beat in the buttermilk, vanilla, and egg just until blended. The batter will not be smooth; do not overbeat.

4. Spread the batter in the pan; sprinkle evenly with the crumbs.

5. Bake until the cake shrinks from the sides of the pan and the crumbs are golden, 40 to 45 minutes. Cool the cake in the pan on a wire rack. Serve warm or at room temperature.

PLUM CRUNCH CAKE

The classic European cake, plaumenkuchen, *combining a simple butter batter with concentric rings of halved prune plums, is the inspiration for this simple yet elegant cake. Serve with a dollop of lightly whipped cream flavored with a pinch of cinnamon and a splash of* slivovitz *brandy. Instead of the plums, you can also use the same weight of fresh apricots or ½ pint fresh raspberries.*

MAKES ONE 8-INCH SQUARE CAKE, 6 TO 8 SERVINGS

The Crunch
½ cup all-purpose flour
⅓ cup sugar
¼ cup (½ stick) unsalted butter, softened
½ teaspoon ground cinnamon

The Cake
½ cup (1 stick) unsalted butter, softened
¾ cup sugar
2 eggs
1 cup all-purpose flour
½ teaspoon baking powder
⅛ teaspoon salt

10 prune plums (about ⅔ pound), halved and pitted

1. Preheat the oven to 350 degrees. Butter an 8-inch square baking pan and set aside.

2. To make the crunch combine the flour, sugar, butter, and cinnamon in a small bowl until the mixture forms big crumbs, then set aside.

3. To make the cake cream the butter in a medium bowl with an electric mixer on high speed until it is light. Gradually add the sugar, a little at a time, and continue beating until the mixture is very light and fluffy. Change the mixer speed to medium and beat in the eggs, one at a time, beating well after each addition.

4. Change the mixer speed to low. Sift the flour, baking powder, and salt into the batter, beating just until blended. Spread the batter in the prepared pan with a spatula, smoothing the top.

5. Arrange the plums skin-side-up, in 5 rows of 4 halves each. Scatter the crumbs over the top.

6. Bake until the crumbs are crisp and crunchy and the plums exude their purple-blue juices, about 1 hour. Serve the cake warm or at room temperature. The cake also freezes very well.

Note. For a 9-inch pan, use the same amount of batter and crumbs, but 15 prune plums, arranged in 5 rows of 6 halves each. The batter can also be baked in 2 6-inch pans.

BLUEBERRY BUCKLE

This softly textured cake is topped with a layer of the berries, which burst during baking and melt into a jamlike consistency, and crowned with crisp golden crumbs. Blackberries and/or raspberries can be substituted for all or part of the blueberries.

MAKES ONE 9-INCH SQUARE CAKE, 9 SERVINGS

The Cake
2 cups all-purpose flour
1 teaspoon baking powder
½ teaspoon salt
½ cup (1 stick) unsalted butter, softened
1 cup sugar
1 egg
¾ cup milk
2¾ cups blueberries, picked over, rinsed, and well drained
½ small lemon

The Crumbs
½ cup sugar
½ cup all-purpose flour
½ teaspoon ground cinnamon
¼ cup (½ stick) unsalted butter, melted

1. Preheat the oven to 350 degrees. Butter a 9-inch square cake pan, then dust with flour and set aside.

2. To make the cake sift together the flour, baking powder, and salt onto a sheet of waxed paper and set aside.

3. In a medium bowl, cream the butter until light with an electric mixer on high speed. Gradually add the sugar and continue beating until the mixture is very light and fluffy. Change the mixer speed to medium and beat in the egg.

4. Change the mixer speed to low. Alternately beat in the sifted dry ingredients and the milk, beginning and ending with the dry ingredients and beating only until combined.

5. Spread the batter in the prepared pan with a spatula, smoothing the top. Scatter the blueberries in an even layer over the batter. Squeeze the lemon juice over the blueberries.

6. To make the crumbs combine the sugar, flour, and cinnamon in a small bowl. Stir in the melted butter until the mixture forms crumbs. Scatter the crumbs in an even layer over the blueberries, pressing them in gently.

7. Bake until the berries burst somewhat and the crumbs are golden, 1 hour and 5 minutes to 1 hour and 10 minutes. Serve warm or at room temperature, cut into squares.

GINGERSNAP CRUMB CAKE

If you can find them, this cake is best when prepared with spicy crisp English or Scandinavian gingersnaps.

MAKES ONE 9-INCH CAKE, 9 TO 12 SERVINGS

The Crumbs
½ cup all-purpose flour
¼ cup firmly packed light or dark brown sugar
1 teaspoon ground ginger
1 teaspoon ground cinnamon
3 tablespoons unsalted butter, softened
¼ cup gingersnap crumbs (about 10 gingersnaps)

The Cake
1¼ cups all-purpose flour
1 teaspoon ground ginger
½ teaspoon ground cinnamon
¾ teaspoon baking powder
½ teaspoon baking soda
½ teaspoon salt
½ cup (1 stick) unsalted butter, softened
1 cup firmly packed light or dark brown sugar
2 eggs
⅓ cup buttermilk

10 × confectioner's sugar, for dusting (optional)

1. Preheat the oven to 350 degrees. Butter a 9 by 9-inch pan and set aside.

2. To make the crumbs combine the flour, brown sugar, ginger, and cinnamon in a medium bowl. Cut in the butter with two knives or a pastry blender, or rub in with your fingers, until the mixture forms a crumbly mass. Stir in the gingersnap crumbs, then set aside.

3. To make the cake sift together the flour, ginger, cinnamon, baking powder, baking soda, and salt onto a sheet of waxed paper and set aside.

4. In a large bowl beat the butter with an electric mixer on high speed until it is light and fluffy. Gradually beat in the brown sugar and continue beating until very light. Change the mixer speed to medium and beat in the eggs, one at a time, beating well after each addition. Change the mixer speed to low and alternately beat in the flour mixture and buttermilk, beginning and ending with the flour mixture and beating just until blended. Spread the batter in the prepared pan and scatter the crumbs over the top, pressing them in lightly.

5. Bake until the top of the cake is firm, the crumbs are crisp, and a skewer inserted in the cake comes out clean, 35 to 40 minutes. Cool in the pan on a wire rack. Dust with the confectioner's sugar before serving, if desired.

PIE PLATE COFFEE CAKE

When time is short, this cake, an adaptation of one given in The Southern Heritage Breads Cookbook, *is easily put together and baked in less than an hour.*

MAKES ONE 9-INCH CAKE, 8 SERVINGS

The Cake
2 cups all-purpose flour
⅓ cup sugar
1½ teaspoons baking powder
½ teaspoon baking soda
¼ teaspoon salt
1 egg
¾ cup buttermilk
½ cup (1 stick) unsalted butter, melted and cooled slightly

The Topping
¼ cup firmly packed light or dark brown sugar
1 tablespoon all-purpose flour
2 teaspoons ground cinnamon
2 tablespoons unsalted butter, softened
½ cup pecans, chopped

The Glaze (optional)
1 cup 10× confectioner's sugar
2 tablespoons milk or cream

1. Preheat the oven to 375 degrees. Butter a 9-inch pie plate and set aside.

2. To make the cake sift together the flour, sugar, baking powder, baking soda, and salt into a large bowl. Add the egg, buttermilk, and melted butter.

3. Beat with the electric mixer on medium speed for 2 minutes, scraping the sides of the bowl with a rubber scraper. Pour the batter into the prepared pan.

4. To make the topping stir together the brown sugar, flour, and cinnamon in a small bowl. Cut in the butter with 2 knives or a pastry blender, or rub in with your fingers, until the mixture forms crumbs. Stir in the pecans, then sprinkle evenly over the batter.

5. Bake until a skewer inserted in the center of the cake comes out clean, about 30 minutes. Let cool in the pan on a wire rack for 15 minutes. Serve the cake warm, or cool completely and drizzle with the optional glaze.

6. To make the glaze beat together the confectioner's sugar and milk in a small bowl until smooth. Drizzle over the cake in any pattern you desire.

CHAPTER 3

LOAF CAKES

Pumpkin, Port, and Ginger Breads

Marzipan Loaves

Quick Cornmeal and Molasses Loaf

Grape-Nuts Bread

Cranberry Bread

Coconut Tea Bread

Roasted Hazelnut–Chocolate Chip Loaf

Banana Tea Loaf

Double Apple Bread

Cinnamon Swirl Loaf

Oatmeal Raisin Loaf

Buttermilk Bran Bread

Peanut Butter Loaf

Cardamom Cream Cake

Apricot Almond Loaf

Walnut Prune Loaf

Date Nut Loaf

Unlike other quick coffee cakes, loaf cakes benefit from being ignored for a day or two before they're sliced. Although they'll taste fine straight from the oven, a bit of time deepens their flavor. When they've been given a chance to age, these straightforward, simple cakes slice better, too. All the better to receive an embellishing spread or butter before serving at breakfast or teatime.

PUMPKIN, PORT, AND GINGER BREADS

Canned pumpkin purée contains pumpkin and nothing else, so I have no qualms about using it instead of the fresh version; it's easy to use, is available year-round, and is consistent in quality. Just be sure to buy pure pumpkin, not the presweetened, prespiced pie filling mix. This recipe makes three big loaves, one for enjoying now, one for freezing and one to give away. If you only want to make one loaf, see the note below. Sandwich thin slices of this spicy loaf with Orange Cream Cheese (page 226).

MAKES THREE 9 BY 5 BY 3-INCH LOAVES

4½ cups all-purpose flour
1 tablespoon baking powder
1½ teaspoons salt
1 teaspoon baking soda
2 teaspoons ground ginger
2 teaspoons ground cinnamon
½ teaspoon ground or freshly grated nutmeg
½ teaspoon ground cloves
1 can (1 pound, 13 ounces) pumpkin purée
6 eggs
1 cup vegetable oil

continued on next page

Pumpkin, Port, and Ginger Breads (*cont.*)

3 cups sugar
1⅔ cups port wine
1 cup chopped walnuts or pecans
½ cup finely chopped crystallized ginger
½ cup golden raisins

1. Preheat the oven to 350 degrees. Butter 3 9 by 5 by 3-inch loaf pans.

2. Into a very large bowl, sift together the flour, baking powder, salt, baking soda, ginger, cinnamon, nutmeg, and cloves.

3. In the workbowl of a large electric food processor, combine the pumpkin, eggs, oil, sugar, and port wine; process until well blended. (If your processor is too small, blend the ingredients half at a time; if you don't have a processor at all, beat everything together in a large bowl.)

4. Pour the pumpkin mixture over the dry ingredients; beat with an electric mixer on high speed or stir with a heavy wooden spoon until well blended. Stir in the nuts, ginger, and raisins. Spread the batter in the loaf pans with a spatula, smoothing the tops.

5. Bake until the loaves begin to pull away from the sides of the pans and a wooden skewer inserted in the center comes out clean, 50 minutes to 1 hour. Cool in the pans on wire racks for 15 minutes, then carefully invert onto the racks, turn right-side-up, and cool completely. The breads slice more neatly if they are wrapped and left for a day or two.

Note. To make one loaf, use 1½ cups flour, 1 teaspoon baking powder, ½ teaspoon salt, ½ teaspoon baking soda, 1 teaspoon each ginger and cinnamon, and ⅛ teaspoon each nutmeg and cloves. For the pumpkin mixture use 1 cup pumpkin purée, 2 eggs, ⅓ cup oil, 1 cup sugar, ⅔ cup port wine, 1 cup nuts, and ½ cup each ginger and raisins.

MARZIPAN LOAVES

Prepared almond paste makes these loaves extra moist and tender. Serve slices, lightly toasted if you like, with Dutch Cocoa Spread (page 227).

MAKES FIVE 4½ BY 2 BY 2-INCH LOAVES

2 cups all-purpose flour
1 teaspoon baking powder
Pinch salt
½ cup (1 stick) unsalted butter
1 can (8 ounces) almond paste
1⅓ cups sugar, plus additional for sprinkling
3 eggs
1 cup milk
¼ cup sliced blanched almonds

1. Preheat the oven to 350 degrees. Butter 5 4½ by 2 by 2-inch loaf pans; dust with flour, tapping out the excess.

2. Onto a sheet of waxed paper, sift together the flour, baking powder, and salt and set aside.

3. In a medium bowl beat the butter and almond paste with an electric mixer on high speed until smooth. Gradually beat in the sugar and continue beating until the mixture is very light.

4. Change the mixer speed to medium. Beat in the eggs, one at a time, beating well after each addition.

5. Change the mixer speed to low. Beat in the flour mixture alternately with the milk, beginning and ending with the flour and beating just until it is incorporated.

6. Divide the batter among the pans, smoothing the tops even with a spatula. Sprinkle with the almonds and additional sugar.

7. Bake until the tops are golden and a skewer inserted in the centers comes out clean, 40 to 45 minutes. Cool in the pans on wire racks 10 minutes, then invert onto the racks, turn right-side-up, and cool completely.

QUICK CORNMEAL AND MOLASSES LOAF

Cornmeal and molasses find themselves together in such classic New England recipes as anadama bread and Indian pudding. This hearty loaf is sweet enough to serve as cake, yet not too overwhelming to be a side dish to a simple supper.

MAKES ONE 9 BY 5 BY 3-INCH LOAF

2 eggs
¼ cup sugar
½ cup molasses
1 cup buttermilk
⅓ cup corn oil
2 cups all-purpose flour
⅓ cup whole-wheat flour
2 teaspoons ground ginger
1½ teaspoons baking powder
¾ teaspoon baking soda
¼ teaspoon salt

1. Preheat the oven to 350 degrees. Butter a 9 by 5 by 3-inch loaf pan and set aside.

2. In a large bowl, beat the eggs with a wire whip until blended. Beat in the sugar, molasses, buttermilk, and oil.

3. Onto a sheet of waxed paper, sift together the flours, ginger, baking powder, baking soda, and salt. With a heavy wooden spoon, stir the dry ingredients into the buttermilk mixture, just until blended. Pour the batter into the prepared pan, smoothing the top with a spatula.

4. Bake until the loaf shrinks from the sides of the pan and a skewer inserted in the center comes out clean, 55 minutes to 1 hour. Let the loaf cool in the pan on a wire rack for 15 minutes, then carefully invert onto the rack and turn right-side-up. Serve the loaf warm (it will not slice very neatly) or at room temperature.

GRAPE-NUTS BREAD

I've always loved the wheaty flavor and gutsy texture of Grape-Nuts cereal. This quick bread captures the cereal's heartiness.

MAKES ONE 9 BY 5 BY 3-INCH LOAF

2 tablespoons wheat germ, for dusting the pan

1 cup raisins
1 cup milk
½ cup honey
½ cup sugar
3 tablespoons unsalted butter
2 cups Grape-Nuts cereal plus additional for sprinkling on the top of the loaf
1 cup whole-wheat flour
1 cup all-purpose unbleached flour
1½ teaspoons baking powder
½ teaspoon baking soda
¼ teaspoon salt
2 eggs
1 teaspoon pure vanilla extract

1. Preheat the oven to 350 degrees. Butter a 9 by 5 by 3-inch loaf pan; dust with the wheat germ and set aside.

2. In a medium saucepan, combine the raisins, milk, honey, sugar, and butter. Bring to a boil over moderate heat. Pour over 1½ cups of the cereal in a large bowl; let cool 15 minutes.

3. Sift the flours, baking powder, baking soda, and salt directly into the bowl; add the remaining ½ cup of cereal, eggs, and vanilla. Stir with a heavy wooden spoon just until blended.

4. Spoon the batter into the prepared pan, smoothing the top. Sprinkle with the remaining cereal.

5. Bake until the loaf shrinks from the sides of the pan and a skewer inserted in the center comes out clean, about 1 hour. Loosely cover the top of the loaf with aluminum foil if it is getting too dark during baking.

6. Cool the loaf in the pan on a wire rack for 20 minutes. Carefully loosen around the sides of the pan, then invert onto the rack and turn right-side-up. Cool completely.

CRANBERRY BREAD

For some people, cranberry bread should be filled with little flecks of the berries; for others, each bite must have whole pieces of the fruit, bursting with tartness. This recipe leaves the choice up to you. Serve slices with Ginger Butter (page 233).

MAKES ONE 9 BY 5 BY 3-INCH LOAF

1 cup walnuts
1½ cups fresh or frozen cranberries (do not thaw if frozen)
2¼ cups all-purpose flour
⅔ cup sugar
2 teaspoons baking powder
1 teaspoon baking soda
½ teaspoon salt
2 teaspoons grated orange zest
1 cup fresh orange juice
⅓ cup vegetable oil
2 eggs, lightly beaten

1. Preheat the oven to 350 degrees. Generously butter a 9 by 5 by 3-inch loaf pan and set aside.

2. For a cranberry-flecked loaf, in the workbowl of an electric food processor, pulse-chop the walnuts and cranberries 12 times. Some of the cranberries will be in big pieces. For a loaf with whole cranberries, pulse-chop only the walnuts. Set the walnuts and cranberries aside.

3. Into a medium mixing bowl, sift together the flour, sugar, baking powder, baking soda, and salt. Make a well in the center.

4. Add the orange zest, juice, oil, and eggs to the well. Stir with a large heavy spoon just until blended; do not overmix. Fold in the walnuts and chopped or whole cranberries. Spoon the batter into the prepared pan, smoothing the top.

5. Bake until the top of the loaf is golden and springy when pressed with a fingertip and a skewer inserted in the center of the loaf comes out clean, about 1 hour and 15 minutes. Cool in the pan on a wire rack for 15 minutes. Gently loosen the cake around the sides of the pan, then invert onto the rack and turn right-side-up. Let cool completely.

6. The loaf is best prepared a day before slicing, but it should be refrigerated or frozen for longer storage.

COCONUT TEA BREAD

A topping of Chocolate Mousse Spread (page 238) or thin slices of fresh pine-apple go nicely with this tea bread.

MAKES TWO 9 BY 5 BY 3-INCH LOAVES

2 cups flaked sweetened coconut
1 cup chopped pecans
4½ cups all-purpose flour
1 tablespoon baking powder
1 teaspoon baking soda
½ teaspoon salt
1 cup (2 sticks) unsalted butter, softened
1 cup sugar
4 eggs
1 can (15 ounces) cream of coconut
1 cup sour cream or plain yogurt

1. Preheat the oven to 350 degrees. In the preheating oven, toast the coconut and pecans in even layers in separate pans, stirring occasionally, until golden, 10 to 15 minutes. Set aside to cool. Butter 2 9 by 5 by 3-inch loaf pans; flour the pans, tapping out the excess, and set aside.

2. Onto a sheet of waxed paper, sift together the flour, baking powder, baking soda, and salt, then set aside.

3. In a large bowl beat the butter until light with an electric mixer on high speed. Gradually beat in the sugar and continue beating until very light and fluffy. Change the mixer speed to medium. Beat in the eggs, one at a time, beating well after each addition.

4. Change the mixer speed to low. Alternately beat in the sifted dry ingredients and the cream of coconut blended with the sour cream or yogurt, beginning and ending with the dry ingredients and mixing just until combined. Fold in the toasted coconut and pecans.

5. Divide the batter between the prepared pans, smoothing the tops with a spatula.

6. Bake until a wooden skewer inserted in the center of the loaves comes out clean, about 1 hour and 10 minutes, loosely covering the tops with aluminum foil if they are browning too quickly. Cool in the pans on a wire rack for 10 minutes. Gently unmold, then turn right-side-up and cool completely. The loaves slice more neatly if they are baked the day before serving.

ROASTED HAZELNUT– CHOCOLATE CHIP LOAF

This is no ordinary tea bread. The flavor and moistness of aromatic hazelnut paste permeates the loaf.

MAKES ONE 9 BY 5 BY 3-INCH LOAF

2 cups hazelnuts (about 11 ounces), roasted and skinned (see *Note*)
1 package (6 ounces) semisweet chocolate pieces
1 cup sugar
1¾ cups all-purpose flour
1¼ teaspoons baking powder
½ teaspoon salt
⅝ cup (1¼ sticks) unsalted butter, softened
1 egg
2 egg yolks
¾ cup sour cream
1 tablespoon dark rum
2 teaspoons pure vanilla extract

1. Preheat the oven to 350 degrees. Butter a 9 by 5 by 3-inch loaf pan and set aside.

2. In the workbowl of a food processor, coarsely pulse-chop ½ cup of the hazelnuts with the chocolate pieces; remove and set aside.

3. Add the remaining 1½ cups of hazelnuts and ½ cup of the sugar to the processor. Cover and process until the mixture forms a peanut butter–like paste, stopping the motor once or twice to scrape the sides of the workbowl with a rubber spatula.

4. Onto a sheet of waxed paper, sift together the flour, baking powder, and salt, then set aside.

5. In a large bowl, cream the butter until light with an electric mixer on high speed. Gradually add the remaining ½ cup sugar and continue beating until the mixture is very light and fluffy. Beat in the hazelnut paste. Change the mixer speed to medium and add the egg and the egg yolks, one at a time, beating well after each addition.

6. Change the mixer speed to low. Alternately beat in the sifted dry ingredients and the sour cream mixed with the rum and vanilla, beginning and ending with the dry ingredients and beating only until combined. Fold in the chopped nuts and chocolate.

7. Spread the batter in the prepared pan, pushing it up around the sides.

8. Bake until a skewer inserted in the center of the loaf comes out clean, 1 hour to 1 hour and 10 minutes. If, after about 50 minutes, the top of the loaf seems to be darkening too quickly, loosely cover it with aluminum foil and continue baking. Let the loaf stand in the pan on a wire rack for 15 minutes. Loosen from the sides of the pan, then carefully invert onto the rack and turn right-side-up. Cool completely before wrapping or serving.

continued on next page

Roasted Hazelnut–Chocolate Chip Loaf (*cont.*)

Note. To roast and skin hazelnuts, place the nuts in a single layer in a roasting or jelly-roll pan. Bake in a 300-degree oven until the skins crack and loosen, the interiors of the nuts are golden, and the nuts are very fragrant. Do not overbake; the nuts will continue to darken once they are removed from the oven due to their interior heat. Place the nuts in a tea towel and fold the towel over to enclose them. Briskly rub the towel back and forth to loosen the skins from the nuts. Remove the nuts from the towel, leaving the skins behind.

BANANA TEA LOAF

For Tropical Ice-Cream Sundaes, toast slices of this intensely flavored loaf, top with vanilla ice cream and toasted coconut, and drizzle with banana liqueur. The recipe doubles easily.

MAKES ONE 9 BY 5 BY 3-INCH LOAF

1 cup banana or vanilla yogurt
⅔ cup sugar
2 eggs
1 teaspoon pure vanilla extract
2 large very ripe bananas
½ cup (1 stick) unsalted butter, melted and cooled slightly
1⅔ cups all-purpose flour
1 teaspoon baking powder

½ teaspoon baking soda
¼ teaspoon salt
¾ cup chopped walnuts, pecans, and/or coconut (optional)

1. Preheat the oven to 350 degrees. Butter a 9 by 5 by 3-inch loaf pan and set aside.

2. In the workbowl of a food processor, combine the yogurt, sugar, eggs, and vanilla. Cover and process until blended. Cut the bananas directly into the processor, add the melted butter, then cover and process until the mixture is almost smooth (a few banana pieces is not only okay but desirable). (Alternatively, beat the yogurt, sugar, eggs, and vanilla until smooth in a medium bowl with the electric mixer on medium speed. Mash the bananas in a small bowl; add to the yogurt.

3. Into a large bowl, sift together the flour, baking powder, baking soda, and salt. Add the banana-yogurt mixture and the optional nuts and/or coconut. Stir just until blended. Spoon the batter in the prepared pan, spreading it a bit higher around the edges.

4. Bake until a skewer inserted in the center of the loaf comes out clean, about 1 hour to 1 hour and 10 minutes.

5. Let the loaf cool in the pan on a wire rack for 20 minutes. Carefully loosen around the sides of the pan, then invert onto the rack and turn right-side-up. Let cool completely before serving.

DOUBLE APPLE BREAD

This abundantly sized loaf gets its well-rounded flavor from a bit of whole-wheat flour and its moistness from applesauce. Although it won't slice neatly, it is delicious enjoyed warm from the oven. For more precise slices, let the loaf rest a day before cutting.

MAKES ONE 9 BY 5 BY 3-INCH LOAF

1 cup walnuts
½ cup (1 stick) unsalted butter, softened
1 cup plus 2 tablespoons firmly packed light brown sugar
2 eggs
1 teaspoon pure vanilla extract
1½ cups unsweetened applesauce
1⅔ cups all-purpose flour
½ cup whole-wheat flour, preferably stoneground
1 teaspoon baking soda
¼ teaspoon salt
1½ teaspoons ground cinnamon
½ teaspoon grated or ground nutmeg
1 large tart apple (such as Granny Smith or Greening), quartered,
    pared, cored, and chopped
½ cup (tightly packed) raisins, plumped if dry (see *Note*)

1. Preheat the oven to 350 degrees. In the preheating oven, toast the walnuts in a single layer in a roasting pan or jelly-roll pan. Coarsely chop and set aside to cool. Butter a 9 by 5 by 3-inch loaf pan and set aside.

2. In a large bowl cream the butter until light with an electric mixer on high speed. Gradually add the sugar and continue beating until the mixture is very light and fluffy. Change the mixer speed to medium. Add the eggs, one at a time, beating well after each addition, then beat in the vanilla and the applesauce. The mixture will look hopelessly curdled. Do not worry!

3. Change the mixer speed to low. Sift in the flours, baking soda, salt, cinnamon, and nutmeg and beat just until combined. Stir in the chopped apple, raisins, and walnuts.

4. Spread the batter in the prepared pan with a spatula, smoothing the top.

5. Bake until a skewer inserted in the center comes out clean, about 1 hour and 30 minutes, loosely covering the top of the loaf with aluminum foil after 50 minutes or so if the loaf seems to be darkening too quickly. Let the loaf stand in the pan on a wire rack for 15 minutes. Loosen from the sides of the pan, then carefully invert onto the rack and turn right-side-up. Cool completely before wrapping or serving.

Note. To plump raisins, place them in a small saucepan with water to cover. Bring to a simmer over moderate heat. Drain thoroughly.

CINNAMON SWIRL LOAF

As this spicy loaf bakes, it fills the kitchen with a heavenly aroma and acquires a crunchy top. Dip day-old slices into a sherry-infused egg batter (just a tablespoon or two will do) for terrific French toast.

MAKES ONE 9 BY 5 BY 3-INCH LOAF

The Cinnamon Swirl
⅓ cup sugar
2 teaspoons ground cinnamon
2 tablespoons unsalted butter, melted

The Batter
1¾ cups all-purpose flour
1¼ teaspoons baking powder
¼ teaspoon baking soda
¼ teaspoon salt
½ cup (1 stick) unsalted butter, softened
¾ cup sugar
2 eggs
2 teaspoons pure vanilla extract
1 cup sour cream

1. Preheat the oven to 350 degrees. Butter a 9 by 5 by 3-inch loaf pan and set aside.

2. To make the cinnamon swirl combine the sugar and cinnamon in a small cup and set aside.

3. To make the batter sift together the flour, baking powder, baking soda, and salt onto a sheet of waxed paper and set aside.

4. In a large bowl cream the butter until light with an electric mixer on high speed. Gradually add the sugar and continue beating until the mixture is very light and fluffy. Change the mixer speed to medium. Add the eggs, one at a time, beating well after each addition, then beat in the vanilla.

5. Change the mixer speed to low. Alternately beat in the sifted dry ingredients and the sour cream, beginning and ending with the dry ingredients and beating only until combined.

6. Spoon half of the batter into the prepared pan. Sprinkle half of the cinnamon mixture over the top. Repeat with the remaining batter and cinnamon sugar. Drizzle the melted butter over the top. To make the swirl, cut through the batter with a table knife several times.

7. Bake until a skewer inserted in the center comes out clean, about 1 hour. Let the loaf stand in the pan on a wire rack for 15 minutes. Loosen from the sides of the pan, then carefully invert onto the rack and turn right-side-up. Cool completely before serving.

OATMEAL RAISIN LOAF

This homey loaf is topped with lightly spiced oatmeal crumbs. It needs no embellishment and has a "nice chew." For economy of effort and flavor, the raisins are plumped and the resulting liquid is used to soften the oats in the batter.

MAKES ONE 9 BY 5 BY 3-INCH LOAF

The Oat Crumb Topping
3 tablespoons old-fashioned oatmeal
2 tablespoons unsalted butter, melted
2 tablespoons all-purpose flour
1 tablespoon firmly packed light brown sugar
½ teaspoon ground cinnamon
¼ teaspoon ground ginger

The Batter
1 cup old-fashioned oatmeal
1½ cups water
1 cup (about 6½ ounces) raisins
1¾ cups all-purpose flour
1¼ teaspoons baking soda
1 teaspoon ground cinnamon
½ teaspoon ground ginger
½ teaspoon salt
½ cup (1 stick) unsalted butter, softened
¾ cup firmly packed light brown sugar

2 eggs
1 teaspoon pure vanilla extract

1. Preheat the oven to 350 degrees. Butter a 9 by 5 by 3-inch loaf pan and set aside.

2. To make the oat crumb topping combine all of the topping ingredients in a small bowl until they form a crumbly mixture and set aside.

3. To make the batter place the oatmeal in a large bowl. In a small saucepan, combine the water and the raisins. Bring to a boil over moderate heat, then remove from the heat. Pour the raisins into a colander or sieve placed over the oatmeal, stirring the liquid into the oats to moisten evenly. Let the oats and raisins stand while preparing the remainder of the batter.

4. Onto a sheet of waxed paper, sift together the flour, baking soda, cinnamon, ginger, and salt and set aside.

5. In a large bowl cream the butter until light with an electric mixer on high speed. Gradually add the sugar and continue beating until the mixture is very light and fluffy. Change the mixer speed to medium. Add the eggs, one at a time, beating well after each addition, then beat in the vanilla and oat mixture.

6. Change the mixer speed to low. Beat in the sifted dry ingredients, just until combined. Stir in the raisins. The batter will be very sticky.

continued on next page

Oatmeal Raisin Loaf (*cont.*)

7. Spoon the batter into the prepared pan. Scatter the crumb topping over the top, pressing it down well into the batter.

8. Bake until a skewer inserted in the center comes out clean, 1 hour to 1 hour and 10 minutes. Cool the loaf in the pan on a wire rack for 15 minutes. Loosen around the sides of the pan, then carefully invert onto the rack and turn right-side-up. Let cool completely before serving.

BUTTERMILK BRAN BREAD

Serve this chewy bread with Whipped Honey Butter (page 232) or a mild cheese. The ripe banana in the batter provides a fruity undertone that deepens if the bread is allowed to mellow in the refrigerator for a day or two.

MAKES ONE 9 BY 5 BY 3-INCH LOAF

1 cup buttermilk
2 very ripe bananas
½ cup sugar
⅓ cup safflower or corn oil
1 egg
1 teaspoon pure vanilla extract
1 teaspoon ground cinnamon
½ teaspoon grated or ground nutmeg

2 cups All-Bran cereal
¼ cup raisins
½ ripe banana, sliced (optional)
1½ cups all-purpose flour
1½ teaspoons baking soda
¼ teaspoon salt
¾ cup chopped walnuts

1. Preheat the oven to 350 degrees. Butter a 9 by 5 by 3-inch loaf pan
   and set aside.

2. In the workbowl of an electric food processor, combine the buttermilk, very ripe bananas, sugar, oil, egg, vanilla, cinnamon, and
   nutmeg. Cover and process until most of the banana is puréed.

3. Put the cereal into a large bowl. Pour the buttermilk mixture over
   it and add the raisins and sliced banana, if used. Stir to combine,
   then let stand 15 minutes.

4. Sift the flour, baking soda, and salt over the mixture. Toss the nuts
   into the bowl. Stir the batter just to combine. Spread in the prepared pan with a spatula, smoothing the top even.

5. Bake until a skewer inserted in the center comes out clean, about
   50 minutes. Let the loaf cool in the pan on a wire rack for 15
   minutes. Loosen around the sides of the pan. Carefully invert onto
   the rack, then turn right-side-up and cool completely. For neat
   slicing and best flavor, wrap the loaf in plastic and let stand for a
   day before slicing.

PEANUT BUTTER LOAF

This loaf slices beautifully, even when it's fresh from the oven. I prefer using natural peanut butter in the recipe; it contains no added sugar or salt, and it is incorporated easily into the other ingredients. Spread slices of this bread with sour cherry or damson plum preserves, for a sophisticated version of peanut butter and jelly.

MAKES ONE 9 BY 5 BY 3-INCH LOAF

2 cups all-purpose flour
½ cup granulated sugar
1¼ teaspoons baking soda
¾ teaspoon baking powder
½ teaspoon salt
½ cup firmly packed light or dark brown sugar
1 cup milk
1 cup peanut or corn oil
1 egg
1 teaspoon pure vanilla extract
1 cup natural peanut butter

1. Preheat the oven to 350 degrees. Butter a 9 by 5 by 3-inch loaf pan and set aside.

2. In a large bowl, whisk together the flour, sugar, baking soda, baking powder, and salt. Stir in the brown sugar.

3. In a small bowl, whisk together the milk, oil, egg, and vanilla. Add to the dry ingredients along with the peanut butter. Stir with a large heavy spoon just until blended. Spread the batter in the prepared pan.

4. Bake until a skewer inserted in the center of the loaf comes out clean, 1 hour to 1 hour and 10 minutes. If, after 50 minutes or so, the top of the loaf seems to be darkening too quickly, loosely cover it with a piece of aluminum foil. Let the loaf cool in the pan on a wire rack for 15 minutes. Loosen around the sides of the pan, then carefully invert onto the rack and turn right-side-up. Cool completely before serving.

CARDAMOM CREAM CAKE

This crunch-topped loaf combines the flavors of café brûlot, the flaming coffee drink, enlivened with spice and orange zest. The crunchy texture remains even when the top of the cake is doused with its orange glaze.

MAKES ONE 9 BY 5 BY 3-INCH LOAF

The Cardamom Sugar
⅓ cup sugar
1 teaspoon ground cardamom
Grated zest of ½ navel orange (about 1½ teaspoons)

The Cake
1¾ cups all-purpose flour
1½ teaspoons baking powder
¼ teaspoon baking soda
¼ teaspoon salt
1 cup sour cream
1 tablespoon instant espresso powder dissolved in 1 tablespoon hot
   water
2 teaspoons pure vanilla extract
½ cup (1 stick) unsalted butter, softened
¾ cup sugar
2 eggs

The Glaze
¼ cup double-strength coffee
Juice of ½ navel orange (about ¼ cup)
2 tablespoons sugar

1. Preheat the oven to 350 degrees. Generously butter a 9 by 5 by 3-inch loaf pan and set aside.

2. To make the cardamom sugar combine the sugar, cardamom, and orange zest in a small cup until well blended and set aside.

3. To make the cake sift together the flour, baking powder, baking soda, and salt onto a sheet of waxed paper and set aside. In a small bowl, stir together the sour cream, dissolved espresso, and vanilla and set aside.

4. In a large bowl, cream the butter until light with an electric mixer on high speed. Gradually add the sugar and continue beating until the mixture is very light and fluffy. Change the mixer speed to medium. Add the eggs, one at a time, beating well after each addition.

5. Change the mixer speed to low. Alternately beat in the sifted dry ingredients and the sour cream mixture, beginning and ending with the dry ingredients and beating only until combined.

6. Spread half of the batter in the prepared pan with a spatula, smoothing the top even. Sprinkle with half of the cardamom sugar, then repeat with the remaining batter and cardamom sugar.

continued on next page

Cardamom Cream Cake (*cont.*)

7. Bake until a skewer inserted in the center of the loaf comes out clean, 1 hour to 1 hour and 10 minutes. If the top of the loaf browns too quickly, loosely cover it with aluminum foil. Let the loaf cool in the pan on a wire rack for 15 minutes. Loosen from the sides of the pan, then carefully invert onto the rack and turn right-side-up.

8. To make the glaze combine the coffee, orange juice, and sugar in a small saucepan. Bring to a simmer over moderate heat; simmer 3 minutes, then brush the glaze over the warm cake. Cool the cake completely before serving.

APRICOT ALMOND LOAF

Dense and moist, this loaf gets its jewellike appearance from the apricots suspended throughout it. The toasted almonds offset the tangy apricots beautifully.

MAKES ONE 9 BY 5 BY 3-INCH LOAF

1 cup whole natural almonds
1 package (11 ounces) dried apricots
1½ cups apricot nectar
½ cup sugar
¼ cup (½ stick) unsalted butter
2 cups all-purpose flour

1½ teaspoons baking powder
½ teaspoon baking soda
¼ teaspoon salt
2 eggs

1. Preheat the oven to 350 degrees. In the preheating oven, toast the almonds in a single layer in a roasting or jelly-roll pan, cool, then chop coarsely. Butter a 9 by 5 by 3-inch loaf pan and set aside.

2. In the workbowl of a food processor, pulse-chop the apricots. Place in a medium saucepan, then add the apricot nectar, sugar, and butter. Bring to a rolling boil over moderate heat, stirring occasionally, until the butter is almost completely melted. Remove from the heat and let cool.

3. Into a medium bowl, sift together the flour, baking powder, baking soda, and salt. Stir in the chopped cooled nuts.

4. Beat the eggs into the cooled apricot mixture, then pour over the flour mixture and mix with a heavy spoon just until blended. Do not overmix. Spoon the batter into the prepared pan, smoothing the top.

5. Bake until a skewer inserted in the center of the loaf comes out clean, about 1 hour. Cool the loaf in the pan on a wire rack for 15 minutes. Loosen from the sides of the pan, then carefully invert onto the rack and turn right-side-up. Cool completely before serving.

WALNUT PRUNE LOAF

Because of the generous amounts of walnuts and prunes in this loaf, it must be cut with a sharp knife. Serve toasted with Whipped Honey Butter (page 232), Ginger Butter (page 233), or Orange Cream Cheese (page 226).

MAKES ONE 9 BY 5 BY 3-INCH LOAF

1½ cups walnuts, divided
1 cup sugar, divided
2 cups all-purpose flour
1½ teaspoons baking powder
¾ teaspoon ground mace
¼ teaspoon salt
½ cup (1 stick) unsalted butter, softened
2 eggs
½ cup prune juice
3 tablespoons dark rum
1 cup coarsely chopped pitted prunes (about 7½ ounces)

1. Preheat the oven to 350 degrees. Butter a 9 by 5 by 3-inch loaf pan and set aside.

2. In the workbowl of a food processor, combine ½ cup of the walnuts with ⅓ cup of the sugar. Cover and process until finely ground.

3. Onto a sheet of waxed paper, sift together the flour, baking powder, mace, and salt and set aside.

4. In a medium bowl cream the butter until light with an electric mixer on high speed. Gradually add the remaining ⅔ cup sugar, then the walnut sugar, and continue beating until the mixture is very light and fluffy. Change the mixer speed to medium. Add the eggs, one at a time, beating well after each addition.

5. Change the mixer speed to low. Alternately beat in the sifted dry ingredients and the prune juice and rum, beginning and ending with the dry ingredients and beating only until combined. Fold in the remaining 1 cup of walnuts and the chopped prunes.

6. Spread the batter in the prepared pan with a spatula, smoothing the top.

7. Bake until a skewer inserted in the center of the loaf comes out clean, 1 hour and 10 minutes to 1 hour and 20 minutes. Let the loaf cool in the pan on a wire rack for 15 minutes. Loosen from the sides of the pan, then carefully invert onto the rack and turn right-side-up. Cool completely before serving.

DATE NUT LOAF

The simmering of the dates before mixing them with the dry ingredients makes this cake extra "datey"!

MAKES ONE 9 BY 5 BY 3-INCH LOAF

1 container (7 ounces) pitted dates, chopped
¾ cup water
½ cup honey
¼ cup sugar
3 tablespoons butter
1 cinnamon stick
2 cups all-purpose flour
1½ teaspoons baking powder
1 teaspoon ground cinnamon
½ teaspoon baking soda
¼ teaspoon salt
1 cup walnut pieces
2 eggs
1 teaspoon pure vanilla extract

1. Preheat the oven to 350 degrees. Butter a 9 by 5 by 3-inch loaf pan and set aside.

2. In a medium saucepan, combine the dates, water, honey, sugar, butter, and cinnamon stick. Bring to a boil over moderate heat. Lower the heat and simmer for 1 minute, or until the butter almost completely melts. Set aside to cool.

3. Into a large bowl, sift together the flour, baking powder, ground cinnamon, baking soda, and salt. Toss in the walnuts.

4. Remove and discard the cinnamon stick from the date mixture, then stir in the eggs and vanilla. Add the mixture to the flour mixture and stir with a heavy spoon just until blended. Do not overmix. Spoon the batter into the prepared pan, smoothing the top.

5. Bake until a skewer inserted in the center of the loaf comes out clean, 50 minutes to 1 hour. Let the loaf cool in the pan on a wire rack for 15 minutes. Loosen from the sides of the pan, then carefully invert onto the rack and turn right-side-up. Cool completely before serving.

CHAPTER 4

SLICING CAKES

Lemon Poppy-Seed Cake

German Chocolate Marble Cake

Hungarian Coffee Cake

Valencia Rum Cake

Cream Cheese Pound Cake

Florida Coconut Pound Cake

Very Vanilla Nut Cake

Dried Sour Cherry Almond Cake

Pecan Parlor Cake

Bourbon Praline Pound Cake

Gianduja Pound Cake

Slicing cakes are just that: Cut them into thin slices and they can be sandwiched with a complementary spread or two. Serve them in wedges with a dollop of cream or a scoop of ice cream, and they become a simple dessert.

In some cases, I've teamed a slicing cake with a suitable glaze. But there's no reason to limit yourself to the topping I've provided. These are adaptable cakes that can be frosted, glazed, or served with an ever-so-light dusting of confectioner's sugar. In fact, though most are simple to prepare, they can be easily gussied up with a quick filling such as a tangy jam, melted chocolate, or peanut butter blended with a bit of crème fraîche and honey.

LEMON POPPY-SEED CAKE

Infusing the poppy seeds in milk before mixing the cake batter releases their nutty flavor but retains their pleasing crunch. This cake is unusual in that it only calls for the whites of eggs, rather than whole eggs or yolks.

MAKES ONE 10-INCH TUBE CAKE

The Cake
1⅓ cups poppy seeds
2¼ cups milk
4½ cups all-purpose unbleached flour
1½ tablespoons baking powder
1 teaspoon salt
6 egg whites
2 cups sugar
1½ cups (3 sticks) unsalted butter, softened
Grated zest of 2 lemons
1½ teaspoons pure vanilla extract

The Lemon Glaze
Juice and coarsely grated zest of 1 lemon
1 tablespoon lemon-flavored or plain vodka
1 to 1½ cups sifted confectioner's sugar

Poppy seeds and lemon zest, for garnish (optional)

continued on next page

Lemon Poppy-Seed Cake (*cont.*)

1. To make the cake combine the poppy seeds and 1 cup of the milk in a small saucepan. Bring to a simmer over moderate heat, then remove from the heat and let stand 30 minutes, or until the seeds absorb most of the milk. (This can be done up to a day ahead; just be sure to cover and refrigerate the poppy seeds until you are ready to use them.)

2. Preheat the oven to 350 degrees. Butter a 10-inch tube pan; dust with flour and tap out the excess.

3. In a medium bowl, stir together the flour, baking powder, and salt.

4. In a small, deep bowl, beat the egg whites with an electric mixer on high speed until they are foamy white and doubled in volume. Beat in ¾ cup of the sugar, 1 tablespoon at a time, until the egg whites form soft peaks.

5. In a large bowl, beat the butter and remaining 1¼ cups sugar with the mixer on high speed until soft and creamy, about 3 minutes. Lower the mixer speed and beat in the poppy seed mixture, lemon zest, and vanilla.

6. Alternately beat in the flour mixture and the remaining milk, beating after each addition just until the batter is smooth.

7. Stir ¼ of the beaten egg whites into the batter, then fold in the remainder. The batter will be very stiff. Pour and spread the batter into the prepared pan, smoothing the top.

8. Bake until a skewer inserted halfway between the edge of the pan and the tube comes out clean, about 1 hour and 15 minutes. Cool in the pan on a wire rack for 30 minutes, then carefully invert the cake onto a rack, turn right-side-up and cool completely.

9. To make the lemon glaze combine the juice and coarsely grated zest of lemon in a small bowl. Add the lemon-flavored or plain vodka. Slowly beat in the confectioner's sugar until a glaze is formed that is thick enough to slowly pour over the cake. Drizzle the glaze over the top of the cake, allowing the excess to flow down the side. Sprinkle with additional lemon zest and poppy seeds, if desired.

GERMAN CHOCOLATE
MARBLE CAKE

Lemon and rum enhance the bittersweet chocolate in this butter-rich cake. The baking soda in the chocolate batter causes the cake to marbleize as it bakes. For a more dramatic marbling, use a table knife to cut down and up through the batter all around the pan, just before placing the cake in the oven.

MAKES ONE 10-INCH TUBE CAKE, 15 TO 20 SERVINGS

9 ounces bittersweet chocolate, finely chopped (see *Note*)
2½ cups all-purpose unbleached flour
2 teaspoons baking powder
Pinch of salt
1½ cups (3 sticks) unsalted butter, at room temperature
1¾ cups sugar
7 eggs, at room temperature
Grated zest and juice of 1 large lemon (about 1 tablespoon zest and
    ¼ cup juice)
5 tablespoons dark rum
3 tablespoons milk
½ teaspoon baking soda

Additional rum and lemon juice for sprinkling on the cake

1. Preheat the oven to 350 degrees. Butter a 10-inch tube pan; dust with flour and tap out the excess.

2. In a small heavy saucepan, melt the chocolate over low heat and set aside.

3. Into a small bowl, sift together the flour, baking powder, and salt and set aside.

4. In a large mixing bowl beat the butter with an electric mixer on high speed until it is light. Gradually beat in the sugar, beating well after each addition, scraping the sides of the bowl. Change the mixer speed to medium. Beat in 2 of the eggs, then 2 more, then the remaining 3, beating only enough after each addition to incorporate them. (The mixture may appear curdled at this point, but this is perfectly okay.)

5. Change the mixer speed to low and beat in the lemon zest and juice and 2 tablespoons of the rum.

6. Gradually beat the flour mixture into the butter mixture, just until it is incorporated. Divide the batter approximately in half by re-moving about 3 cups to a small bowl.

7. In a cup, stir together the remaining 3 tablespoons of rum with the milk, then stir in the baking soda. Gradually add this mixture to the melted chocolate. (The chocolate may thicken slightly.) Stir the melted chocolate mixture into one half of the batter.

8. Spoon the chocolate batter into the prepared pan, spreading evenly with a rubber spatula. With a clean spoon and spatula,

continued on next page

German Chocolate Marble Cake (*cont.*)

place the lemon batter over the chocolate batter, smoothing the top.

9. Bake until a skewer inserted halfway between the edge of the pan and the tube comes out clean, about 1 hour. Let the cake cool in the pan on a wire rack for 20 minutes. Carefully loosen the cake from the sides and tube of the pan and invert onto a second wire rack. Turn the cake right-side-up and let cool completely on the rack. Sprinkle the cake with additional rum and lemon juice. Store in a tightly covered tin at room temperature, or freeze the cake and bring it to room temperature before serving. (The cake may also be refrigerated, but it must be brought back to room temperature before serving or it will have a dry, heavy consistency.)

Note. Use three 3-ounce bars of chocolate, a generous ½ pound of chopped bittersweet chocolate, or 1½ cups semisweet chocolate pieces.

HUNGARIAN COFFEE CAKE

I'm not sure whether the notion of tucking layers of nuts, dried fruit, chocolate, and jam within a cake batter originated in Hungary or not. There is a strong resemblance between the filling for this cake and those of the pastry-wrapped cookie, rugelach. In any event, this is a cake with European nuances.

MAKES ONE 10-INCH TUBE CAKE, 16 SERVINGS

The Filling
½ cup dried cherries
⅓ cup Cherry Heering or other cherry liqueur plus additional for
  batter, if needed
2 tablespoons sugar
1 bar (3 ounces) semisweet or bittersweet chocolate, *or* ½ cup
  semisweet chocolate pieces
1 tablespoon cocoa powder (not a mix)
½ teaspoon ground cinnamon
½ cup unchopped walnuts
1 tablespoon cherry preserves, preferably from sour cherries

continued on next page

Hungarian Coffee Cake (*cont.*)

The Cake
3 cups all-purpose flour
2½ teaspoons baking powder
1 teaspoon baking soda
½ teaspoon salt
1 cup sour cream
1½ teaspoons pure vanilla extract
1 cup (2 sticks) unsalted butter, softened
1 cup sugar
4 eggs

1. To make the filling combine the dried cherries and the liqueur in a small bowl. Cover and let stand at least 4 hours, or overnight, stirring occasionally.

2. Drain the cherries, reserving the thickened liqueur. Place the sugar, chocolate, cocoa, and cinnamon in the workbowl of a food processor. Cover and pulse-chop until the chocolate is in pea-size pieces. Add the nuts, drained cherries, and preserves. Pulse-chop until the nuts and cherries are coarsely chopped, then set aside. (The filling can be prepared up to a week in advance; just be sure to cover and store in a cool place or in the refrigerator.)

3. To make the cake preheat the oven to 350 degrees. Butter a 10-inch tube pan; flour the pan, tapping out the excess, and set aside.

4. Onto a sheet of waxed paper, sift together the flour, baking powder, baking soda, and salt and set aside. Measure the reserved liqueur and add more liqueur to yield ⅓ cup. Combine the sour cream and the liqueur with the vanilla and set aside.

5. In a large bowl beat together the butter and the sugar with an electric mixer on high speed until very light. Change the mixer speed to medium. Beat in the eggs, one at a time, beating well after each addition.

6. Change the mixer speed to low. Alternately add the dry ingredients and the sour cream mixture to the butter mixture, beginning and ending with the dry ingredients and mixing just until combined.

7. Spoon about ⅓ of the batter into the prepared pan and dot with ½ of the cherry-chocolate mixture. Repeat this layering and top with the last ⅓ of the batter, smoothing the top.

8. Bake until a skewer inserted in the center of the cake comes out clean, about 1 hour. Cool the cake in the pan on a wire rack for 10 minutes, then invert the cake onto the rack and turn right-side-up; cool completely.

VALENCIA RUM CAKE

Soaked in an orange rum syrup, this cake is moist and rich enough to be served plain, or it can be topped with a bittersweet chocolate glaze or split and sandwiched with sweet orange marmalade or apricot preserves.

MAKES ONE 9-INCH TUBE CAKE

The Cake
2½ cups all-purpose flour
2 teaspoons baking powder
1 teaspoon baking soda
½ teaspoon salt
1 cup (2 sticks) unsalted butter, softened
1 cup sugar
3 eggs
1 tablespoon grated orange zest (from 2 navel oranges)
1 teaspoon grated lemon zest (from 1 lemon)
1 cup buttermilk

The Glaze
Juice of 1 navel orange (about ½ cup)
Juice of ½ lemon (about 2 tablespoons)
¼ cup plus 2 tablespoons sugar
2 tablespoons dark rum

1. Preheat the oven to 350 degrees. Butter a 9-inch tube pan and set aside.

2. To make the cake sift together the flour, baking powder, baking soda, and salt onto a sheet of waxed paper and set aside.

3. In a large bowl beat the butter with an electric mixer on high speed until light. Gradually beat in the sugar and continue beating until very light and fluffy. Change the mixer speed to medium. Beat in the eggs, one at a time, beating well after each addition, then beat in the orange and lemon zests.

4. Change the mixer speed to low. Alternately beat in the sifted dry ingredients and buttermilk, beginning and ending with the dry ingredients and beating just until combined. Spoon the batter into the prepared pan, smoothing the top.

5. Bake until the cake shrinks from the sides and tube of the pan, the top is springy when lightly pressed with a fingertip, and a skewer inserted halfway between the sides and the tube comes out clean, about 1 hour.

6. Cool the cake in the pan on a wire rack for 15 minutes. Carefully loosen from the pan, then invert onto the rack and turn right-side-up. Let cool to room temperature.

7. To make the glaze combine the orange and lemon juices, sugar, and rum in a small saucepan. Bring to a boil over moderate heat, then remove from the heat. Place the cake on a plate. Spoon and

continued on next page

Valencia Rum Cake (*cont.*)

brush the glaze all over the cake, letting the excess run down the sides; it will soak into the bottom. Let stand for 1 hour.

8. Loosely cover the cake with aluminum foil. Let stand for a day, if possible, before serving to allow the flavors to blend.

CREAM CHEESE POUND CAKE

You won't perceive the cream cheese in this closely textured cake, but you will notice the moist, tender quality and ultimate sliceability it bestows. Sometimes I sprinkle the just-baked cake with a few drops of raspberry brandy or peach schnapps, which makes the cake especially nice when it's served alongside fresh berries in the summertime.

MAKES ONE 9-INCH TUBE CAKE, 12 SERVINGS

1½ cups all-purpose flour
1 teaspoon baking powder
¼ teaspoon salt
¾ cup (1½ sticks) unsalted butter, softened
4 ounces cream cheese, softened
1¼ cups sugar
4 eggs
2 teaspoons pure vanilla extract

1. Preheat the oven to 350 degrees. Butter a 9-inch tube pan; flour the pan, tapping out the excess, and set aside.

2. Onto a sheet of waxed paper, sift together the flour, baking powder, and salt and set aside.

3. In a large bowl cream the butter and cream cheese with an electric mixer on high speed until light. Gradually add the sugar and continue beating until the mixture is very light and fluffy. Change the mixer speed to medium. Add the eggs, one at a time, beating well after each addition, then beat in the vanilla.

4. Change the mixer speed to low. Beat in the sifted dry ingredients, beating only until combined. Spread the batter in the prepared pan, smoothing the top even.

5. Bake until the cake shrinks from the sides and tube of the pan, the top is springy when lightly pressed with a fingertip, and a skewer inserted halfway between the sides and tube comes out clean, about 50 minutes to 1 hour.

6. Cool the cake in the pan on a wire rack for 15 minutes. Carefully loosen the cake around the sides and tube with a sharp knife, then carefully invert onto the rack and turn right-side-up. Cool completely.

Variation. To make a tangerine pound cake, add 2 teaspoons grated tangerine zest to the batter along with the vanilla. Brush the just-baked cake with a syrup of ½ cup tangerine juice and ⅓ cup sugar, simmered for 1 minute.

FLORIDA COCONUT
POUND CAKE

This sunny yellow cake gets its intense color from orange rind, orange juice, and eggs. Very dense and rich, it should be cut into thin slivers. Since zest should be grated from an orange before it's juiced, grate what you'll need for both the cake and the glaze before you squeeze the juice.

MAKES ONE 10-INCH TUBE CAKE, 24 SERVINGS

The Cake
4 cups all-purpose flour
2 teaspoons baking powder
1 teaspoon baking soda
½ teaspoon salt
1½ cups (about 3 ¾ ounces) flaked coconut
2 cups (4 sticks) unsalted butter, softened
2 cups sugar
8 eggs
2 tablespoons grated orange zest (from 2 navel oranges)
1¼ cups freshly squeezed orange juice (from 5 navel oranges)

The Orange Glaze
1 cup 10 × confectioner's sugar, sifted
1 tablespoon grated orange zest (from 1 navel orange)
¼ cup freshly squeezed orange juice (from 1 navel orange)
1 tablespoon freshly squeezed lemon juice

2 tablespoons toasted flaked coconut, for the top of the cake (optional)

1. To make the cake preheat the oven to 350 degrees. Butter a 10-inch tube pan; flour the pan, tapping out the excess, and set aside.

2. Onto a sheet of waxed paper, sift together the flour, baking powder, baking soda, and salt. Toss in the coconut and set aside.

3. In a large bowl cream the butter with an electric mixer on high speed until light. Gradually add the sugar and continue beating until the mixture is very light and fluffy. Change the mixer speed to medium. Add the eggs, one at a time, beating well after each addition, then beat in the orange zest. The mixture may look curdled, but this is nothing to worry about.

4. Change the mixer speed to low. Alternately beat in the sifted dry ingredients and the orange juice, beginning and ending with the dry ingredients and beating only until combined. Pour the batter into the prepared pan.

5. Bake until the cake is golden brown on top and a skewer inserted halfway between the sides and tube of the pan comes out clean, about 1 hour and 25 minutes. Cool the cake in the pan on a wire rack for 15 minutes, then carefully invert the cake onto the rack and turn right-side-up.

6. To make the orange glaze beat together the glaze ingredients in a small bowl until smooth and well blended. Place the warm cake on a plate and spoon the glaze over it. Sprinkle with the toasted coconut, if desired. Let the cake cool completely before serving.

VERY VANILLA NUT CAKE

This cake is fortified with both pulverized vanilla bean and vanilla extract. Serve it alone, or pair it with White Chocolate Nut Spread (page 237) or Chocolate Mousse Spread (page 238). Chocolate Satin Glaze (page 194) is also a suitable flourish.

MAKES ONE 9-INCH TUBE CAKE, 12 SERVINGS

½ vanilla bean, cut in quarters (see *Note*)
1¼ cups sugar
½ cup hazelnuts, toasted and skinned (page 13)
½ cup pecans
2¼ cups all-purpose flour
1½ teaspoons baking powder
½ teaspoon baking soda
½ teaspoon salt
¾ cup (1½ sticks) unsalted butter, softened
4 eggs
¾ cup milk
1 teaspoon pure vanilla extract

1. Preheat the oven to 350 degrees. Butter a 9-inch tube pan; flour the pan, tapping out the excess, and set aside.

2. In the workbowl of a food processor, combine the vanilla bean pieces with ½ cup of the sugar. Process until the vanilla is ground up. Some pieces of the vanilla bean will remain; although they

will be further broken up during mixing, they can be removed, if desired, by sifting the sugar. Set the vanilla sugar aside.

3. Place the hazelnuts and pecans in the processor. Cover and pulse-chop until some of the nuts are ground and the remainder is chopped, then set aside.

4. Onto a sheet of waxed paper, sift together the flour, baking powder, baking soda, and salt, then set aside.

5. In a large bowl cream the butter with an electric mixer on high speed until light. Gradually add the vanilla sugar, then the remaining sugar, and continue beating until the mixture is very light and fluffy. Change the mixer speed to medium and add the eggs, one at a time, beating well after each addition.

6. Change the mixer speed to low. Alternately beat in the sifted dry ingredients and the milk and vanilla extract, beginning and ending with the dry ingredients and beating only until combined. Fold in the chopped nuts.

7. Spread the batter in the prepared pan with a spatula, smoothing the top even.

8. Bake until skewer inserted halfway between the sides and tube of the pan comes out clean, about 1 hour. Cool in the pan on a wire rack for 15 minutes, then carefully invert onto the rack, turn right-side-up, and cool completely.

Note. I use a Bourbon vanilla bean from Madagascar, available through the Williams-Sonoma Company. The vanilla is intoxicatingly fragrant and so fresh that it resembles a dried fruit.

DRIED SOUR CHERRY ALMOND CAKE

This cake uses both ground blanched almonds and toasted natural almonds with their skins on.

MAKES ONE 10-INCH TUBE CAKE, 20 SERVINGS

The Cake
1 cup blanched whole almonds
2 cups sugar
2⅔ cups all-purpose flour
1 teaspoon baking powder
1 teaspoon baking soda
½ teaspoon salt
1 cup (2 sticks) unsalted butter, softened
6 eggs
2 tablespoons kirsch or cherry liqueur
1 cup sour cream
1 cup whole almonds, toasted, cooled, and chopped
1 cup dried sour cherries

The Glaze (optional)
1 to 1½ cups sifted 10× confectioner's sugar
1 to 3 tablespoons milk
1 tablespoon kirsch

1. Preheat the oven to 350 degrees. Butter a 10-inch tube pan and set aside.

2. To make the cake place the blanched almonds and 1 cup of the sugar in the workbowl of a food processor. Cover and process until the almonds are ground, then set aside.

3. Onto a sheet of waxed paper, sift together the flour, baking powder, baking soda, and salt and set aside.

4. In a large bowl cream the butter with an electric mixer on medium speed until light. Gradually add the remaining 1 cup of sugar, then the almond sugar, and continue beating until the mixture is very light and fluffy. Add the eggs, 2 at a time, beating well after each addition. Beat in the kirsch.

5. Change the mixer speed to low. Alternately beat in the sifted dry ingredients and the sour cream, beginning and ending with the dry ingredients and beating only until combined. Stir in the chopped almonds and dried cherries.

6. Spoon the batter into the prepared pan, smoothing the top.

7. Bake until the top of the cake is golden brown, a skewer inserted halfway between the sides of the pan and the tube comes out clean, and the top is springy, about 1 hour and 15 minutes. If the top of the cake appears to be darkening too quickly, loosely cover it with a piece of aluminum foil and continue baking.

8. Let the cake cool in the pan on a wire rack for 30 minutes, then carefully loosen around the sides and tube of the pan and invert
continued on next page

Dried Sour Cherry Almond Cake (*cont.*)
   onto the rack; turn right-side-up and cool completely.

9. If desired, sprinkle the cake with a few drops more kirsch, or, to make the glaze, combine the sifted confectioner's sugar, milk, and kirsch in a small bowl until smooth and drizzle it over the completely cooled cake.

PECAN PARLOR CAKE

A simple slicing cake with a hint of orange.

MAKES ONE 10-INCH TUBE CAKE, 12 SERVINGS

2½ cups all-purpose flour
2 teaspoons baking powder
½ teaspoon baking soda
½ teaspoon salt
2 teaspoons pure vanilla extract
1 tablespoon grated orange zest (from 1 navel orange)
1 cup sour cream
1 cup unsalted butter, softened
1 cup granulated sugar
1 cup firmly packed light brown sugar
4 eggs
1½ cups pecans, ground or very finely chopped

1. Preheat the oven to 350 degrees. Butter a 10-inch tube pan and set aside.

2. Onto a sheet of waxed paper, sift together the flour, baking powder, baking soda, and salt. Stir the vanilla and the orange zest into the sour cream. Set the sifted dry ingredients and the sour cream aside.

3. In a large bowl cream the butter with an electric mixer on high speed until light. Gradually add the granulated, then the brown sugars and continue beating until the mixture is very light and fluffy. Change the mixer speed to medium. Add the eggs, one at a time, beating well after each addition.

4. Change the mixer speed to low. Alternately beat in the sifted dry ingredients and the sour cream, beginning and ending with the dry ingredients and beating only until combined. Beat in the ground pecans.

5. Spread the batter in the prepared pan with a spatula, smoothing the top even.

6. Bake until a skewer inserted halfway between the sides of the pan and the tube comes out clean, about 1 hour.

7. Cool the cake in the pan on a wire rack for 15 minutes. Carefully loosen the cake around the side of the pan and the tube, then unmold onto the rack and let cool completely.

BOURBON PRALINE POUND CAKE

The mellow flavor of brown sugar permeates this cake, which is nice dressed up with butter pecan ice cream and caramel sauce.

MAKES ONE 10-INCH TUBE CAKE, 20 SERVINGS

The Cake
3 cups all-purpose flour
1 teaspoon baking powder
½ teaspoon baking soda
½ teaspoon salt
2 tablespoons bourbon
1 teaspoon pure vanilla extract
1 cup heavy or whipping cream
1½ cups (3 sticks) unsalted butter, softened
1 package (1 pound) dark brown sugar, minus ⅓ cup for glaze
4 eggs

The Bourbon Glaze (optional)
1 cup 10× confectioner's sugar
⅓ cup firmly packed dark brown sugar, from 1-pound package (above)
¼ cup (½ stick) unsalted butter
3 tablespoons bourbon

1. To make the cake preheat the oven to 325 degrees. Generously butter a 10-inch tube pan and set aside.

2. Onto a sheet of waxed paper, sift together the flour, baking powder, baking soda, and salt. Add the bourbon and the vanilla to the cream and set aside along with the sifted dry ingredients.

3. In a large bowl cream the butter with an electric mixer on high speed until light. Gradually add the brown sugar and continue beating until the mixture is very light and fluffy. Change the mixer speed to medium. Add the eggs, one at a time, beating well after each addition.

4. Change the mixer speed to low. Alternately beat in the sifted dry ingredients and the cream mixture, beginning and ending with the dry ingredients and beating only until combined.

5. Spread the batter in the prepared pan with a spatula, smoothing the top even.

6. Bake until a skewer inserted halfway between the sides of the pan and the tube comes out clean, about 1 hour and 5 minutes.

7. Cool the cake in the pan on a wire rack for 15 minutes. Carefully loosen the cake around the sides of the pan and tube, then unmold onto the rack and turn right-side-up. Let cool completely.

8. To make the glaze combine all of the glaze ingredients in a small saucepan. Cook over moderately low heat, stirring often, until the sugar dissolves and the glaze is smooth. Drizzle the glaze over the cooled cake and let stand until the glaze sets.

GIANDUJA POUND CAKE

I've always loved the combination of ground hazelnuts and chocolate, whether it's in the melt-in-your-mouth Italian confection known as gianduja, or this deeply flavored cake named in its honor. Look for sweetened praline paste in specialty food shops, or order it from Dean and DeLuca.

MAKES ONE 10-INCH FLUTED TUBE CAKE, 12 SERVINGS

The Cake
4 squares (1 ounce each) unsweetened chocolate
1 ¾ cups all-purpose flour
1 ½ teaspoons baking soda
¼ teaspoon salt
1 cup (2 sticks) unsalted butter, softened
1 cup commercial praline paste
1 cup sugar
4 eggs
1 tablespoon rum
1 teaspoon pure vanilla extract

The Gianduja Glaze (optional)
2 bars (3 ounces each) bittersweet chocolate, chopped
⅓ cup praline paste
¼ cup milk
2 tablespoons unsalted butter
1 tablespoon rum

1. To make the cake preheat the oven to 350 degrees. Butter a 10-inch fluted tube pan and set aside.

2. In a small heavy saucepan over low heat, or in the microwave, melt the unsweetened chocolate and set aside.

3. Onto a sheet of waxed paper, sift together the flour, baking soda, and salt.

4. In a large bowl cream the butter and the praline paste with an electric mixer on high speed until light. Gradually add the sugar and continue beating until the mixture is very light and fluffy. Change the mixer speed to medium. Add the eggs, one at a time, beating well after each addition, then beat in the melted choco-late, rum, and vanilla.

5. Change the mixer speed to low. Beat in the sifted dry ingredients only until combined. The batter will be thick.

6. Spread the batter in the prepared pan with a spatula, smoothing the top even.

continued on next page

Gianduja Pound Cake (*cont.*)

7. Bake until the top of the cake is springy when lightly pressed with a fingertip, the side of the cake recedes from the side of the pan, and a skewer inserted halfway between the sides and the tube of the pan comes out clean, about 50 to 55 minutes. (The top may crack; this is okay.)

8. Cool the cake in the pan on a wire rack for 15 minutes. Carefully loosen the cake around the sides of the pan and the tube, then unmold onto the rack and turn right-side-up. Let cool completely.

9. To make the gianduja glaze combine the chocolate, praline paste, milk, butter, and rum in a small heavy saucepan. Cook over low heat, stirring constantly, until the chocolate melts and the mixture is smooth. Remove from the heat and drizzle over the cooled cake.

CHAPTER 5

FRESH FRUIT CAKES

Ginger-Pear Upside-Down Cake
Three-Berry Coffee Cake
Banana Walnut Coffee Cake
Cranberry Apple Torte
Persimmon Cake
Sour Cherry Crumb Cake
Peach Cake
Ligita's Latvian Apple Cake
Nick Malgieri's Pineapple Crumb Cake
Apricot-Orange Cake
Harvest Apple Cake
Blueberry Corn Cake
Pear-Mincemeat Cake
Strawberry-Rhubarb Cake

Fresh fruit elevates a cake, adding a tangy-sweet character, as well as providing natural color and texture. From winter's tart green apples to summer's bounty of berries, I find the array of possibilities exciting and almost endless. (I have yet to prepare a kiwi crumb cake or a loquat loaf!)

As with crumb cakes that contain fruit, many of these cakes can be prepared with fruits other than those specified. Additionally, a small handful of a complementary fruit can be added to the one called for.

If you're particularly fond of a certain fruit, bake and freeze one or two extra cakes when that fruit is in season. That way you'll be able to savor its elusive flavor regardless of the calendar.

Although coffee cakes are usually a great way to salvage fruit too ripe for eating, remember this caveat: All baked fruit preparations spoil easily, so the cakes must be eaten swiftly, or refrigerated or frozen until serving time.

GINGER-PEAR UPSIDE-DOWN CAKE

Silken pears, crisp walnuts, and a toffeelike glaze top a moist gingerbread base. Served with lightly whipped cream, this cake is a homey autumn dessert. On its own, it is a deliciously different breakfast pastry.

MAKES ONE 9-INCH CAKE

The Fruit Topping
3 firm, ripe pears (about 1½ pounds)
1 quart water, mixed with 2 tablespoons lemon juice
¼ cup (½ stick) unsalted butter
⅓ cup firmly packed dark brown sugar
¾ cup walnut pieces

The Gingerbread Batter
¾ cup (1½ sticks) unsalted butter
3 extra-large eggs
½ cup milk
2¼ cups all-purpose flour
¾ cup firmly packed dark brown sugar
1 tablespoon ground ginger
1½ teaspoons ground cinnamon
½ teaspoon ground cloves
1½ teaspoons baking powder
½ teaspoon salt

continued on next page

Ginger-Pear Upside-Down Cake (*cont.*)

1. Preheat the oven to 350 degrees.

2. To make the fruit topping halve, core, and peel the pears. Place in a bowl with the water and lemon juice; set aside while preparing the rest of the topping and batter.

3. Melt the butter in a 9-inch square baking pan over low heat. Add the brown sugar. Cook, stirring constantly, for about 3 minutes, or until the sugar melts into the butter (don't worry if the mixture looks curdled). Remove from the heat and scatter the walnuts evenly over the glaze; set aside.

4. To make the gingerbread batter melt the butter. In a small bowl, beat the eggs and milk; slowly beat in the butter.

5. Rub the flour, brown sugar, ginger, cinnamon, cloves, baking powder, and salt through a sieve into a large bowl. Pour the egg mixture over the dry ingredients and mix with a large spoon just until blended. The batter will be quite thick.

6. Drain the pears and pat dry with paper towels. Cut the halves lengthwise into ½-inch slices. Place all but the end pieces from each half in 3 rows in the pan. Scatter the remaining little pieces over the top. Gently spread the batter evenly over the pears.

7. Bake until the topping bubbles up around the sides of the pan and the cake is firm and starting to crack, 45 to 50 minutes.

8. Cool the cake in the pan on a wire rack for 10 minutes, then carefully invert onto a large plate and turn right-side-up. Serve warm with whipped cream or ice cream, if desired. Refrigerate the cake if you won't be serving it within a day.

THREE-BERRY COFFEE CAKE

This cake celebrates summer's bounty, when berries are not worth their weight in gold. In less plentiful times, use the same quantity of only one or two types of berries, either fresh or individually quick frozen.

MAKES ONE 10-INCH TUBE CAKE

1½ cups sour cream
1½ teaspoons baking soda
1 teaspoon vanilla
3¼ cups all-purpose unbleached flour
1¾ teaspoons baking powder
Large pinch salt
¾ cup (1½ sticks) unsalted butter, softened
1¼ cups sugar
3 eggs
¾ cup fresh blueberries, rinsed and well drained
¾ cup fresh blackberries, rinsed and well drained
¾ cup fresh raspberries, rinsed and well drained

1. Preheat the oven to 350 degrees. Butter a 10-inch tube pan; dust with flour, tapping out the excess, and set aside.

2. In a small bowl, mix the sour cream, baking soda, and vanilla. Onto a sheet of waxed paper, sift together the flour, baking powder, and salt and set aside along with the sour cream mixture.

3. In a large bowl cream the butter with an electric mixer on high speed until it is light. Gradually beat in the sugar and continue beating until the mixture is light and fluffy. Change the mixer speed to medium and beat in the eggs, one at a time, beating well after each addition.

4. In a small bowl, gently toss the berries with ¼ cup of the sifted flour mixture.

5. Change the mixer speed to low. Alternately beat the remaining sifted dry ingredients and sour cream mixture into the butter mixture, beginning with the dry ingredients and beating just until combined. Very gently fold in the berries, then pour the batter into the prepared pan.

6. Bake until a skewer inserted halfway between the sides and the tube of the pan comes out clean, about 1 hour and 10 minutes. Cool in the pan on a wire rack for 30 minutes, then carefully invert onto the rack and turn right-side-up. Cool completely before serving.

BANANA WALNUT COFFEE CAKE

I find that bananas add both sweetness and moisture to coffee cakes. Overripe bananas that are too soft for eating are ideal for this recipe. Although the cake is delicious served warm, it slices better when it has cooled.

MAKES ONE 10-INCH TUBE CAKE

The Walnut and Sugar Sprinkle
1½ cups chopped walnuts
⅓ cup sugar
1 tablespoon ground cinnamon

The Banana Batter
2 cups all-purpose flour
1 tablespoon baking powder
¼ teaspoon salt
1 cup (2 sticks) unsalted butter, softened
2 cups sugar
2 eggs
1 cup sour cream
2 ripe bananas, mashed, plus 1 firm, ripe banana, for slicing
1 tablespoon pure vanilla extract

10× confectioner's sugar (optional)

1. Preheat the oven to 350 degrees. Butter a 10-inch tube pan; dust with flour, tapping out the excess, and set aside.

2. To make the walnut and sugar sprinkle combine the walnuts, sugar, and cinnamon in a small bowl and set aside.

3. To make the banana batter sift together the flour, baking powder, and salt onto a sheet of waxed paper and set aside.

4. In a large bowl cream the butter with an electric mixer on high speed until it is light. Gradually beat in the sugar and continue beating until light and fluffy. Change the mixer speed to medium. Beat in the eggs, one at a time, beating well after each addition, then beat in the sour cream, mashed ripe bananas, and the vanilla.

5. Change the mixer speed to low. Beat in the flour mixture, just until blended.

6. Spoon half of the batter into the prepared pan. Scatter half of the walnut and sugar sprinkle over the batter. Thinly slice the third banana over the batter. Top with the remaining batter and scatter the remaining walnut and sugar sprinkle over the top.

7. Bake until a skewer inserted halfway between the sides and the tube of the pan comes out clean, about 1 hour and 15 minutes. Let cool in the pan on a wire rack for 20 minutes. Carefully loosen the cake from the sides and tube of the pan, then invert onto a wire rack and turn right-side-up. Serve warm or cool, sprinkled with sifted confectioner's sugar, if desired.

CRANBERRY APPLE TORTE

Here is an adaptation of a recipe given to me by my friend, Nancy Osher, who usually uses tart green apples. The batter bakes up around the sunburst-patterned fruit. The honey in the batter enhances the honeyed undertones of the apples, while the cranberries add both color and piquancy. This is a great cake to make for a Thanksgiving gathering.

MAKES ONE 9-INCH CAKE, 8 SERVINGS

⅓ cup sugar
⅓ cup honey
¾ stick unsalted butter, softened
1 egg
½ cup whole-wheat flour
½ cup all-purpose flour
½ teaspoon ground cinnamon
⅛ teaspoon ground cloves
½ teaspoon baking powder
¼ teaspoon baking soda
¼ teaspoon salt
2 large or 3 small tart apples (about ¾ pound)
¾ cup plus ⅓ cup fresh or frozen whole cranberries
1 tablespoon sugar mixed with ½ teaspoon ground cinnamon and a
    large pinch ground cloves, for the top

1. Preheat the oven to 350 degrees. Generously butter a 9-inch springform pan and set aside.

2. Beat the sugar, honey, and butter until they are well blended and fluffy. Beat in the egg.

3. Stir together the flours, cinnamon, cloves, baking powder, baking soda, and salt; add to the creamed butter mixture and beat in just until blended.

4. Peel and core the apples. Chop enough apple to yield ½ cup and slice the remainder. Add the chopped apple and ¾ cup cranberries to the batter. Beat to break down the apples and cranberries slightly, about 1½ minutes.

5. Spread the batter in the prepared pan. Arrange the sliced apples in a ring about 1 inch from the sides of the pan. Scatter the remaining ⅓ cup cranberries over the top, then sprinkle with the sugar and spice mixture.

6. Bake until the cake shrinks from the sides of the pan, and its top is deep golden and very springy when lightly pressed with a fingertip, about 1 hour.

7. Cool in the pan on a wire rack for 15 minutes. Run a small sharp knife around the edges of the cake, gently remove the sides of the pan, then transfer the cake onto the rack to cool completely.

PERSIMMON CAKE

The persimmon is a curious fruit. When eaten on its own, it has a unique, almost chalky texture that is not to everyone's liking. When used in baking, its flavor imparts a subtle backdrop to the other ingredients, and makes the batter dense and moist. This cake is equally at home on its own with just a dusting of confectioner's sugar, topped with a circle of whipped cream rosettes, or split and filled with lemon or spice buttercream. It's also good with softly whipped rum-flavored heavy cream, into which you've marbled some additional persimmon purée and a tablespoon of minced crystallized ginger.

MAKES ONE 9-INCH CAKE

3 very ripe persimmons (about 7 ounces each)
¾ stick unsalted butter, softened
¾ cup firmly packed dark brown sugar
2 eggs
1½ cups all-purpose unbleached flour
1½ teaspoons ground ginger
1 teaspoon baking soda
½ teaspoon baking powder
¼ teaspoon salt
1 tablespoon dark rum
½ cup chopped walnuts or pecans
⅓ cup golden raisins

1. Preheat the oven to 350 degrees. Generously butter a 9-inch springform pan and set aside.

2. Halve 2 of the persimmons; carefully scoop out the flesh (a grapefruit spoon makes this easy) into the workbowl of a food processor or electric blender, discarding any seeds or large fibers. Cover and process until smooth. Transfer to a 1-cup measure; you should have a scant cup. Halve and scoop out the flesh from the remaining persimmon into the processor or blender; cover and process with on-and-off pulses, just until chopped. Set the purée and chopped persimmon aside.

3. In a bowl beat the butter with an electric mixer at high speed until it is creamy. Gradually beat in the sugar and continue beating until the mixture is light and fluffy, about 1 minute. Beat in the eggs, scraping down the bowl with a rubber spatula.

4. Sift together the flour, ginger, baking soda, baking powder, and salt. Alternately add the flour mixture, persimmon purée, and the rum to the mixing bowl, beginning and ending with the flour mixture. The batter will be thick. Fold in the chopped persimmon, nuts, and raisins. Spread the batter in the prepared pan with a spatula, smoothing the top.

5. Bake until the cake shrinks from the sides of the pan and its top is deep golden-brown and springy when lightly pressed with a fingertip, about 45 to 50 minutes.

6. Cool in the pan on a wire rack for 15 minutes. Run a small sharp knife around the edges of the cake and the sides of the pan, then remove onto the rack to cool completely.

SOUR CHERRY CRUMB CAKE

The short season for sour cherries makes their flavor all the more special. Here, they're sandwiched between a macadamia batter and macadamia-studded crumbs. If desired, blanched almonds can be substituted for the macadamias.

MAKES ONE 9-INCH CAKE

1 pound sour cherries, rinsed, stemmed, and pitted (about 2 cups)

The Crumbs
¼ cup (½ stick) unsalted butter
½ cup sugar
½ cup all-purpose flour
¾ teaspoon ground cinnamon
¼ cup macadamia nuts (about 1 ounce), finely chopped

The Cake
½ cup (1 stick) unsalted butter, at room temperature
¾ cup sugar
1 egg
⅓ cup sour cream
1 teaspoon pure vanilla extract
Few drops almond extract
½ cup (about 2 ounces) macadamia nuts, ground
1½ cups all-purpose flour
1 teaspoon baking powder

¼ teaspoon salt
1 tablespoon dry bread crumbs

1. Preheat the oven to 350 degrees. Butter a 9-inch springform pan and set aside.

2. Place the cherries in a colander set over a bowl; let them drain while preparing the crumbs and batter (this prevents sogginess in the cake).

3. To make the crumbs combine the butter, sugar, flour, cinnamon, and nuts in a small bowl until blended; set aside.

4. To make the cake beat the butter in a medium bowl with an electric mixer on high speed until it is light and fluffy; gradually beat in the sugar and continue beating until well blended. Change the mixer speed to medium. Beat in the egg, then the sour cream, vanilla and almond extracts, and nuts. Change the mixer speed to low. Sift in the flour, baking powder, and salt, and mix just until combined.

5. Spread the batter in the prepared pan, building up the sides slightly. Sprinkle the bread crumbs in the hollow formed by the batter. Arrange the cherries in an even layer over the batter, pressing them in lightly.

6. Sprinkle the crumbs in an even layer over the cherries, pressing them in gently.

continued on next page

Sour Cherry Crumb Cake (*cont.*)

7. Bake until the crumbs are crisp and the top of the cake is golden, about 1 hour. Let stand in the pan on a wire rack for 20 minutes. Carefully loosen the cake around the edges of the cake and the sides of the pan, then remove onto the rack to cool completely.

PEACH CAKE

This is a nice summer morning cake, an orange-sparked batter studded with peaches plus a handful of blueberries, if you have them. "Dead-ripe" peaches are ideal here, since they're extra sweet and tender. Just be sure to refrigerate the cake if you won't be eating it within a few hours of baking, since it will spoil very quickly. If you wish, the batter can also be baked in muffin pans.

MAKES ONE 9-INCH CAKE, 12 SERVINGS

The Cake
2 cups all-purpose flour
⅔ cup sugar
1 teaspoon baking powder
1 teaspoon baking soda
¼ teaspoon salt
¾ pound ripe peaches
½ cup vegetable oil
1 egg

2 teaspoons grated orange zest (from 1 navel orange)
½ cup orange juice (from 1 navel orange)
1 cup blueberries (optional)

The Cinnamon Sugar Topping
1 tablespoon sugar
¼ teaspoon ground cinnamon

1. Preheat the oven to 350 degrees. Oil a 9-inch square baking pan and set aside.

2. To make the cake sift together the flour, sugar, baking powder, baking soda, and salt onto a sheet of waxed paper and set aside.

3. Peel and pit the peaches. Cut them up directly into a medium bowl (you should have about 1½ cups). Add the oil, egg, orange zest and juice, and blueberries, if used.

4. Add the flour mixture and gently stir with a large spoon just until blended. Spread the batter in the prepared pan.

5. To make the cinnamon sugar topping stir together the sugar and cinnamon in a small bowl and sprinkle over the batter.

6. Bake until the batter is firm on top and the cake pulls away from the sides of the pan, about 45 to 50 minutes. Cool in the pan on a wire rack. Serve the cake warm or at room temperature.

LIGITA'S LATVIAN APPLE CAKE

Richard Sax enthusiastically contributed the recipe for this clafouti-like cake that he received years ago from playwright Karolyn Nelke. "Almost like a quick apple pie without the crust," it takes just 6 minutes to assemble for the oven. To save even more time, you can eliminate browning the butter, although it does add a particularly mellow flavor.

MAKES ONE 9½-INCH ROUND CAKE, 8 SERVINGS

¾ cup (1½ sticks) unsalted butter

3 medium-size tart apples, such as Granny Smiths or Greenings, peeled, quartered, cored, and sliced

1 teaspoon lemon juice

2 tablespoons plus ¾ cup sugar, plus more as needed

2 teaspoons ground cinnamon (or use a mixture of cinnamon, allspice, and nutmeg)

2 eggs, lightly beaten

1 cup sifted all-purpose unbleached flour

Vanilla ice cream or frozen yogurt, for serving (optional)

1. In a small saucepan over moderate heat, melt the butter; continue cooking until lightly golden, about 7 minutes. Watch carefully to avoid burning. Pour the butter into a medium mixing bowl, leaving behind any darkened sediment in the pan.

2. Preheat the oven to 350 degrees. Generously butter a deep 9½-inch pie pan (or use a 10-inch pan or rustic ceramic oval gratin dish). Toss the apple slices in a bowl with the lemon juice, the 2 tablespoons sugar, and the cinnamon. Spread the apples evenly in the buttered pan.

3. Stir the ¾ cup sugar into the browned butter. Gently stir in the eggs, mixing until smooth. Add the flour and stir gently just until blended; don't overmix. Pour this batter over the apples; it should cover them fairly evenly, but it's fine if a few apple pieces show through. Sprinkle the surface with about 1 tablespoon more sugar.

4. Bake until the cake is lightly golden and crusty, 40 to 45 minutes. Cool briefly on a wire rack, then cut into wedges and serve warm, topped with vanilla ice cream or frozen yogurt, if you like.

NICK MALGIERI'S PINEAPPLE CRUMB CAKE

Nick Malgieri, noted pastry chef and cookbook author, often substitutes fresh apricots, sour cherries, peaches, or prune plums for the pineapple in this moist cake. Melted butter imparts extra crispness to the crumbs.

MAKES ONE 10-INCH CAKE, 10 TO 12 SERVINGS

The Cake
½ cup (1 stick) unsalted butter, softened
¾ cup sugar
1 egg
3 egg yolks
1 teaspoon pure vanilla extract
1¼ cups unbleached all-purpose flour
1 teaspoon baking powder
1 medium pineapple (about 2 to 2½ pounds), to yield about 3 cups sliced

The Crumbs
1¼ cups unbleached all-purpose flour
½ cup sugar
¼ teaspoon ground cinnamon
½ cup (1 stick) unsalted butter, melted

1. To make the cake, preheat the oven to 350 degrees. Butter a 10-inch round cake pan, 2 inches deep, and line the bottom of the pan with a round of parchment paper or waxed paper; set aside.

2. In a large bowl beat the butter and the sugar with an electric mixer on high speed until soft and light. Add the egg and continue beating until light, then add the yolks, one at a time, beating well after each addition. Beat in the vanilla.

3. Sift together the flour and baking powder, and stir into the batter. Spread the batter evenly in the prepared pan.

4. Pare the skin from the pineapple with a serrated knife. Quarter, core, and cut the pineapple in ½-inch slices. Arrange the pineapple on the batter in concentric rows, overlapping slightly, leaving a margin of about 1 inch around the edge. Don't be concerned if the pineapple mounds slightly in the center of the cake; the top will even out as the cake bakes.

5. To make the crumbs mix the flour, sugar, and cinnamon in a small bowl. Stir the melted butter into the mixture and rub with your fingers to make coarse crumbs.

6. Scatter the crumbs over the pineapple and the batter as evenly as possible.

7. Bake until a knife inserted in the center comes out clean, about 1 hour. Cool the cake in the pan on a wire rack for 15 minutes, then invert onto a plate and unmold the cake; remove the paper. Invert the rack onto the cake, turn the cake right-side-up, and cool completely before serving.

APRICOT-ORANGE CAKE

Fresh orange zest enlivens fresh apricots, which are often a bit lackluster in flavor.

MAKES ONE 9-INCH CAKE, 10 SERVINGS

½ cup (1 stick) unsalted butter, softened
¾ cup firmly packed light brown sugar
4 eggs
2 teaspoons grated orange zest (from 1 navel orange)
2 tablespoons orange liqueur
1 teaspoon pure vanilla extract
1⅔ cups all-purpose flour
1 teaspoon baking powder
¼ teaspoon salt
12 firm ripe apricots, halved and pitted (about 1¾ pounds)
2 tablespoons granulated sugar

10× confectioner's sugar, for sprinkling on baked cake
1 tablespoon shredded orange zest, for sprinkling on baked cake

1. Preheat the oven to 350 degrees. Butter a 9-inch springform pan; dust with flour, tapping out the excess, and set aside.

2. In a medium bowl beat the butter and brown sugar with an electric mixer on high speed until light and creamy. Change the mixer speed to medium. Beat in the eggs, one at a time, beating well after each addition. Beat in the orange zest, orange liqueur, and vanilla.

3. Change the mixer speed to low. Sift the flour, baking powder, and salt into the batter, mixing just until blended.

4. Spread the batter in the prepared pan. Arrange the apricots, cut-side-up, in concentric rings on top of the batter, lightly pressing them into the batter. Sprinkle the 2 tablespoons of granulated sugar over the apricots.

5. Bake until the top of the cake is firm when lightly pressed with a fingertip and the cake begins to pull away from the sides of the pan, about 35 minutes.

6. Let the cake cool in the pan on a wire rack for 20 minutes. Carefully loosen the cake around the sides of the pan with a sharp knife, then dust with the confectioner's sugar and sprinkle with shredded orange zest. Remove the pan. Serve the cake warm or at room temperature. The cake is best eaten within a day of baking.

HARVEST APPLE CAKE

This open-face apple cake is an adaptation of one created by my friend Mary Jo Wilfong. Served with a dollop of Calvados-flavored whipped cream, it makes a comforting winter dessert. Served on its own, it fits into both brunch and teatime menus. If desired, the apple slices can be left unpeeled.

MAKES ONE 9 BY 13-INCH CAKE

The Cake
1 cup (2 sticks) unsalted butter
3 cups all-purpose flour
1½ cups sugar
1 tablespoon baking powder
2 teaspoons ground cinnamon
½ teaspoon salt
4 eggs
½ cup milk
4 teaspoons pure vanilla extract
½ cup raisins (optional)
3 large tart apples

The Topping
⅔ cup firmly packed light brown sugar
Ground cinnamon

1. Preheat the oven to 350 degrees. Butter a 9 by 13-inch baking pan and set aside.

2. To make the cake melt the butter; remove and reserve ¼ cup for the topping.

3. Into a large bowl, sift together the flour, sugar, baking powder, cinnamon, and salt. Add the remaining ¾ cup butter, eggs, milk, and vanilla.

4. Beat with an electric mixer on medium speed, scraping the sides of the bowl with a rubber spatula several times, for 2 minutes or until blended. Scrape the butter into the prepared pan, smoothing the top. Scatter the raisins, if used, over the batter.

5. Quarter and core the apples. Leave the peel on or pare, as you wish. Cut the apples into ⅓-inch-thick slices. Arrange the apples in rows over the batter in the pan.

6. To make the topping gently brush some of the reserved melted butter over the apples. Sprinkle half of the brown sugar over the top, then dust liberally with the cinnamon. Drizzle the remaining butter over the sugar, then sprinkle with the remaining sugar.

7. Bake until the apples are tender, the cake shrinks from the sides of the pan, and a skewer inserted in the center comes out clean, about 1 hour. Cool in the pan on a wire rack. Cut while still warm, using a sharp knife.

Note. The recipe can be baked in 2 8-inch square baking pans for 50 minutes to 1 hour.

BLUEBERRY CORN CAKE

Blueberries and cornmeal are combined in cakes of many permutations. This one is a grainy, lemon-scented pound cake. The cornmeal in the batter makes a sunny backdrop to the bursts of blueberries throughout. If allowed to rest overnight, the cake slices beautifully, even into paper-thin slices. It should not, however, be left at room temperature for more than a few hours, since blueberries seem to spoil very quickly.

MAKES ONE 9-INCH TUBE CAKE, 12 SERVINGS

2½ cups plus 3 tablespoons all-purpose flour
1 teaspoon baking powder
1 teaspoon baking soda
½ teaspoon salt
½ cup yellow cornmeal
1 cup (2 sticks) unsalted butter, softened
1½ cups sugar
4 eggs
2 teaspoons grated lemon zest
⅔ cup buttermilk
1 pint blueberries, picked over, rinsed, and well drained

1. Preheat the oven to 350 degrees. Butter a 9-inch tube pan; flour the pan, tapping out the excess, and set aside.

2. Into a medium bowl, sift together 2½ cups of flour with the baking powder, baking soda, and salt. Stir in the cornmeal and set aside.

3. In a large bowl, cream the butter with an electric mixer on high speed until light. Gradually add the sugar and continue beating until the mixture is very light and fluffy. Change the mixer speed to medium. Add the eggs, one at a time, beating well after each addition, then beat in the lemon zest.

4. Change the mixer speed to low. Alternately beat in the sifted dry ingredients and the buttermilk, beginning and ending with the dry ingredients and beating only until combined.

5. In a small bowl, toss the blueberries with the 3 tablespoons of flour. Gently fold into the batter, trying not to crush the berries more than necessary. Spoon the batter into the prepared pan, smoothing the top even.

6. Bake for 1 hour. Loosely cover the top of the pan with aluminum foil and continue baking for 30 minutes longer, or until a skewer inserted halfway between the sides of the pan and the tube comes out clean.

7. Cool the cake in the pan on a wire rack for 15 minutes. Carefully loosen the cake from the sides of the pan and the tube, then invert onto the rack, turn right-side-up, and cool completely.

PEAR-MINCEMEAT CAKE

This cake uses up that last bit of mincemeat from the holiday pantry, combining it with its classic fruit partner, the buttery pear. The brandy, lemon, and pears will uplift even the most mundane of prepared mincemeats. Golden delicious apples would be a good substitute for the pears.

MAKES ONE 9-INCH CAKE, 8 SERVINGS

The Cake
1 cup mincemeat
½ cup chopped ripe pear
2 tablespoons cognac or brandy
1 teaspoon grated lemon zest
1 tablespoon freshly squeezed lemon juice
½ cup (1 stick) unsalted butter
¾ cup sugar
1 egg
1½ cups all-purpose unbleached flour
¾ teaspoon baking powder
½ teaspoon baking soda
¼ teaspoon salt

The Topping
2 firm, ripe pears
1 teaspoon freshly squeezed lemon juice
1 tablespoon sugar

1. Preheat the oven to 350 degrees. Generously butter a 9-inch springform pan and set aside.

2. To make the cake combine the mincemeat, chopped pear, cognac or brandy, lemon zest, and lemon juice in a small bowl and set aside.

3. In a bowl, beat the butter with an electric mixer at high speed until it is creamy. Gradually beat in the sugar and continue beating until the mixture is light and fluffy, about 1 minute. Beat in the egg, scraping down the bowl with a rubber spatula. Beat in the mincemeat-pear mixture and continue beating for about 30 seconds, to break up the pears a bit. The batter will look hopelessly curdled, but do not worry.

4. Sift the flour, baking powder, baking soda, and salt into the bowl. Beat with the mixer on high speed just until the flour mixture is absorbed. Spread the batter into the prepared pan, smoothing the top even.

5. Pare, halve, core, and cut the pears lengthwise into ⅓-inch-thick slices. Place the pear slices, spoke-fashion, about 1 inch from the edges of the pan. Sprinkle the pears with the lemon juice, then the sugar.

6. Bake until the cake shrinks from the sides of the pan, its top is deep golden and very springy when lightly pressed with a fingertip, and the pears are tender, about 1 hour and 5 minutes.

7. Cool in the pan on a wire rack for 15 minutes. Run a small sharp knife around the edges of the pan, then gently remove the side of the pan. Serve warm or at room temperature.

STRAWBERRY-RHUBARB CAKE

This rosy cake resembles a giant Swedish pancake, with its center of fruit filling surrounded by an impressive puff of batter. Plan to serve the cake within a day of baking it, since the fruit tends to make it soggy after that.

MAKES ONE 9-INCH CAKE, 8 TO 10 SERVINGS

The Fruit Filling
2 cups sliced rhubarb (about ½ pound) (cut into ½ by ¾-inch slices)
1 cup sliced hulled strawberries (about ½ pint)
⅓ cup sugar
1½ tablespoons cornstarch
1 tablespoon dry bread crumbs
¼ teaspoon grated orange zest

The Almond Paste Batter
1½ cups all-purpose flour
1 teaspoon baking powder
¼ teaspoon salt
½ cup (about 5 ounces) almond paste
½ cup sugar
½ cup (1 stick) unsalted butter, softened
2 eggs
2 teaspoons grated orange zest

½ cup sour cream
1 tablespoon dry bread crumbs

The Glaze
Juice of 1 navel orange (about ⅓ cup)
Accumulated syrup from the filling

Unhulled strawberry halves and 10× confectioner's sugar, for garnishing (optional)

1. Preheat the oven to 350 degrees. Butter a 9-inch springform pan and set aside.

2. To make the fruit filling combine all of the filling ingredients in a small bowl, tossing gently to mix. Let stand for 20 to 30 minutes while preparing the cake batter.

3. To make the almond paste batter sift together the flour, baking powder, and salt onto a sheet of waxed paper and set aside.

4. In a medium bowl, beat together the almond paste and sugar with an electric mixer on low speed until they form fine crumbs. Add the butter, ¼ at a time, and continue beating until creamy and free of lumps.

5. Beat in the eggs, one at a time, beating well after each addition, then beat in the orange zest. Alternately beat in the sifted dry ingredients and the sour cream, beating just until blended. Spread

continued on next page

Strawberry-Rhubarb Cake (*cont.*)

the batter in the prepared pan, sloping it around the edge to form a border.

6. Sprinkle the bread crumbs in the center depression. Transfer the strawberry-rhubarb filling to the center of the batter with a slotted spoon, leaving a ¾-inch border all around and reserving the accumulated syrup for the glaze.

7. Bake until the top of the cake is golden brown and the cake pulls away from the sides of the pan, 1 hour to 1 hour and 10 minutes. Let cool completely in the pan on a wire rack.

8. To make the glaze bring the orange juice to a boil in a small saucepan over moderate heat. Add the reserved strawberry-rhubarb juices. Simmer until the glaze thickens.

9. Brush the fruit filling with the glaze. Just before serving, brush it with the glaze once again. Dust the border of the cake with the confectioner's sugar and decorate with the fresh strawberry halves, if desired. Serve slices of the cake immediately after cutting them.

Variation. The almond paste base can be used with a filling of blueberries and/or peaches, too.

CHAPTER 6

SPECIAL-OCCASION CAKES

Cheesecake Coffee Cake

Kugelhopf—The Quick Way

Hawaiian Coconut Coffee Cake

Cranberry Relish Cake

Chocolate Chip Cookie Cake

Arabian Nights Cake

Holiday Preserves Cake

Classic Sour Cream Coffee Cake

Coconut Tunnel of Fudge Cake

Bountiful Honey Cake

Poppy Nut Cake

Date Orange Cake

Maple Walnut Sticky Cake

Bienenstich

Caramel Espresso Swirl Cake

Chocolate Walnut Cake
Nina's Almond Torte
Light and Spicy Gingerbread
One-Bowl Apple Spice Cake
One-Bowl Carrot Cake

What constitutes a special occasion? The obvious answer is birthdays, anniversaries, and other milestones. The holidays are predictable, too. Sometimes, however, a plain old ordinary day inspires one to bake something other than the usual.

There's a time and a place for multitiered extravaganzas, festooned with rosettes of buttercream. But not all special-occasion cakes require such elaborate treatment. A dense chocolate walnut cake enrobed with a satiny chocolate glaze is classy without being fancy. A traditional sour cream cake makes any day special. In fact, there are many times when a less complex creation is more appropriate and more desirable.

Special-occasion coffee cakes are usually rich with generous amounts of butter, sugar, and eggs and they are often embellished with a simple but elegant glaze. Although suave cousins to crumb cake and tea loaves, they are still easy to prepare.

CHEESECAKE COFFEE CAKE

The name says it all. A graham cracker crumb crust surrounds a buttery-rich cake with a tunnel of lemon-spiked cheese filling punctuated with plump dried currants. During baking, the cheese filling sinks to the bottom of the pan, where it nestles under the crumbs. This cake is rich. Cut it in ½-inch-pieces with a serrated knife.

MAKES ONE 12-INCH TUBE CAKE, 12 TO 15 SERVINGS

The Crust
2 cups graham cracker crumbs
¼ cup sugar
¼ cup all-purpose flour
½ cup (1 stick) unsalted butter, melted

The Cheese and Currant Filling
⅓ cup dried currants
12 ounces cream cheese, softened
½ cup sugar
2 egg yolks
1 tablespoon all-purpose flour
1 teaspoon grated lemon zest
4 teaspoons fresh lemon juice

continued on next page

Cheesecake Coffee Cake (*cont.*)

The Batter
1¾ cups all-purpose flour
1½ teaspoons baking powder
½ teaspoon salt
1½ sticks unsalted butter, softened
1 cup sugar
3 eggs
½ cup milk
1 teaspoon pure vanilla extract

1. Preheat the oven to 350 degrees.

2. To make the crust, butter a 12-inch tube pan. In a small bowl, combine the graham cracker crumbs, sugar, and flour. Drizzle the butter over the top and stir with a spoon until well blended. Carefully and evenly press the crumbs into the bottom and at least halfway up the sides and tube of the pan. Set the pan aside.

3. To make the cheese and currant filling place the currants in a small saucepan and add water to cover. Bring to a boil over moderate heat. Drain the currants in a colander set over the sink; let cool while preparing the rest of the filling.

4. In a small bowl, beat the cream cheese until it is creamy. Beat in the sugar, egg yolks, flour, lemon zest and juice, then the cooled currants; set aside.

5. To make the batter sift together the flour, baking powder, and salt. In a bowl, beat the butter with an electric mixer on high speed until it is creamy. Slowly beat in the sugar, then the eggs. Alternately beat in the flour mixture and the milk and vanilla, beginning and ending with the flour mixture. The batter may appear curdled; do not worry.

6. Working gently to avoid dislodging the crumb crust, spoon the batter into the pan, smoothing the top even. With the back of a small spoon, make a 1-inch-deep depression in the center of the batter, all around the pan. Spoon the cheese filling into the depression; some of it will overflow on top of the batter.

7. Bake until the top of the cake is golden brown, firm, and springy to the touch and the cake shrinks from the sides and tube of the pan, about 1 hour and 10 minutes. Cover the top of the cake with aluminum foil during baking if it is getting too dark. The top of the cake may crack and appear to be too soft.

8. Cool the cake in the pan for about 20 minutes. Carefully invert onto a wire rack covered with a piece of waxed paper or aluminum foil (this will catch any crumbs that fall off the cake). Cool the cake crumb-side-up.

KUGELHOPF—
THE QUICK WAY

This is the kind of Continental-style cake that inspires long afternoons of sipping tea with schnapps, listening to classical music, and watching the world go by. It was inspired by two recipes that appeared in Paula Peck's classic book, The Art of Fine Baking. *Both her German Sand Torte and Melting Tea Cake use lemon zest in a tender Genoise-like batter. I've added golden raisins and slivered almonds to give the cake kugelhopf-like character. If you use a standing mixer with a wire whip attachment, you'll get the best results. For best flavor and texture, plan on baking the cake a day before serving it. The cake is also delicious toasted.*

MAKES ONE 9-INCH TUBE CAKE

1 cup golden raisins
½ cup dark rum
¼ cup dry bread crumbs
16 to 18 whole blanched almonds (optional)
1 cup unsalted butter
4 eggs
2 egg yolks
1 cup sugar
1¾ cups all-purpose flour
½ teaspoon baking powder
¼ teaspoon salt

⅔ cup blanched slivered almonds
1 teaspoon grated lemon zest
1½ teaspoons vanilla extract
10 × confectioner's sugar

The Rum Glaze (optional)
1 cup 10 × confectioner's sugar
1 tablespoon fresh lemon juice
1 tablespoon dark rum

1. Combine the raisins and the rum in a glass or ceramic pie dish; cover and let stand for at least 1 hour, stirring once or twice. (The raisin and rum mixture can be prepared a day ahead.)

2. Preheat the oven to 350 degrees. Generously butter a 9-inch tube pan. Sprinkle the bread crumbs evenly around the sides and tube of the pan, tapping out the excess. Nestle a whole almond in each swirl of the pan's bottom, if desired (the almonds will just peek out through the batter when the cake is unmolded). Set the pan aside.

3. Melt the butter and set aside to cool to room temperature.

4. In a bowl, whisk the eggs and egg yolks with an electric mixer. Slowly whisk in the sugar in a slow steady stream. Place the bowl over a saucepan of simmering water, and heat, whisking constantly, until the eggs are hot and the sugar melts, about 5 minutes.

continued on next page

Kugelhopf—The Quick Way (*cont.*)

5. Remove the bowl from the pan; place on the electric mixer fitted with the wire whip. Beat on high speed until the eggs are at room temperature and tripled in volume, about 7 minutes.

6. Meanwhile, drain the raisins in a sieve set over the butter, thereby adding the rum to the melted butter. Sift together the flour, baking powder, and salt. Remove ⅓ cup of the mixture and add to the raisins in the sieve along with the almonds; toss to coat the raisins and almonds, letting the excess flour sift back onto the remaining flour mixture. Add the lemon zest and vanilla to the butter mixture.

7. Working quickly, fold about ⅓ of the remaining flour mixture into the egg batter. Remove about 1 cup of the batter; stir into the butter mixture. Alternately fold the remaining flour and butter mixtures into the batter, beginning and ending with the flour mixture. Fold in the raisins and almonds. Pour the batter into the prepared pan.

8. Bake until the batter is springy to the touch, the cake shrinks from the sides and tube of the pan, and the top is golden brown, about 1 hour. Cool in the pan on a wire rack 10 minutes; carefully unmold onto the rack, turn right-side-up, and cool completely.

9. Dust the cooled cake with the confectioner's sugar, or drizzle the Rum Glaze over the top.

10. To make the rum glaze mix the confectioner's sugar, lemon juice, and dark rum in a small bowl until smooth and well blended. Drizzle the glaze over the cooled cake placed on a wire rack. Let stand until the glaze sets.

HAWAIIAN COCONUT COFFEE CAKE

This recipe was given to me by Richard Sax, who acquired it from Simon Waters, a former pastry chef in Hawaii. The combination of canned cream of coconut and grated coconut makes it incredibly moist and "coconutty," and the cornstarch gives it a lovely texture.

MAKES ONE 9½-INCH CAKE

The Cake
¾ cup (1½ sticks) unsalted butter, softened
1 cup sugar
1¾ cups unbleached all-purpose flour
¼ cup cornstarch
1 teaspoon baking powder
1 teaspoon baking soda
Pinch salt
3 eggs
1½ teaspoons pure vanilla extract
1¼ cups plain low-fat yogurt or sour cream
¾ cup grated coconut, preferably unsweetened

continued on next page

Hawaiian Coconut Coffee Cake (*cont.*)

The Coconut Glaze
⅓ cup canned cream of coconut, such as Coco Lopez
2 teaspoons cold water

1. Preheat the oven to 350 degrees. Generously butter a 9½-inch or 10-inch springform pan and set aside. (*Note:* You can also bake the cake in 2 6-inch round cake pans; line these with rounds of parchment or waxed paper cut to fit; then butter the paper and sides of the pans well.)

2. To make the cake beat the butter and sugar in a large bowl with an electric mixer on medium-high speed until very light, 6 to 8 minutes. Meanwhile, sift the flour, cornstarch, baking powder, baking soda, and salt onto a sheet of waxed paper and set aside. Add the eggs to the creamed butter mixture, one at a time, then add the vanilla.

3. Add the flour mixture and yogurt or sour cream alternately to the creamed butter mixture, beginning and ending with the flour. Gently pour the batter into the prepared pan, smoothing the surface gently with a spatula. Sprinkle with the coconut and bake until the cake is golden and a toothpick inserted in the center comes out clean, about 50 to 55 minutes (35 to 48 minutes for the 6-inch cakes). Lay a sheet of aluminum foil loosely over the top of the cake if, after about 20 minutes, it seems to be browning too quickly.

4. Cool the cake in the pan on a wire rack for 15 minutes, then carefully run the blade of a sharp knife around the sides of the cake. Remove the springform pan. (For the 6-inch cakes, carefully invert the cakes onto a wire rack set over a sheet of waxed paper, then gently invert them right-side-up again to cool.)

5. To make the coconut glaze heat the cream of coconut and water in a small saucepan over medium heat, stirring, just until the mixture is warm. Poke a fork or a thin skewer gently all over the surface of the cake. While the cake is still warm, slowly spoon the warm glaze over the entire surface of the cake. (If you have inverted the cakes, sprinkle any coconut that has fallen off back onto the glazed surfaces.) Cool the cake completely before serving.

CRANBERRY RELISH CAKE

If you've got a cup of cranberry relish left over from the holidays, tuck it into this orange-spiked cake. A cup of mincemeat can be used in place of the relish, if you wish.

MAKES ONE 10-INCH TUBE CAKE

½ cup (1 stick) unsalted butter
1 cup sugar
2 eggs
Grated zest of 1 navel orange (about 2 teaspoons)
Juice of 1 navel orange (about ⅓ cup)
1 cup plain yogurt
2 cups all-purpose flour
1 teaspoon baking powder
1 teaspoon baking soda
½ teaspoon salt
1 cup chopped walnuts or pecans
1 cup whole-berry cranberry relish, drained if very liquidy

1. Preheat the oven to 350 degrees. Butter the sides and tube of a 10-inch tube pan and set aside.

2. In a large bowl, beat the butter with an electric mixer on high speed until light. Gradually beat in the sugar and continue beating until very light and fluffy. Change the mixer speed to medium. Beat in the eggs, one at a time, then the orange zest and juice, and yogurt. The mixture may appear curdled, but do not worry.

3. Change the mixer speed to low. Sift in the flour, baking powder, baking soda, and salt, and beat just until blended. Stir in half of the nuts.

4. Spread half of the batter in an even layer in the pan. Gently spread the cranberry relish in an even layer over the top, then sprinkle with the remaining nuts. Spread the remaining batter over the top with a spatula, smoothing the top.

5. Bake until the top of the cake is golden and the cake pulls away from the sides and tube of the pan, about 55 minutes. Let cool in the pan on a wire rack for at least 20 minutes before inverting onto the rack to cool completely.

CHOCOLATE CHIP COOKIE CAKE

This chip-studded cake is an adaptation of one created by the Nestlé Company. A crisp, cookielike nut crust provides a nice counterpoint to the moist cake. If you're in a rush, you can omit the crunch altogether and add 1 cup of chopped walnuts along with the chocolate chips. For an accompaniment, what could be better than a tall glass of cold milk?

MAKES ONE 10-INCH TUBE CAKE, 18 SERVINGS

The Nut Crunch
⅜ cup (¾ stick) unsalted butter, softened
½ cup sugar
¼ cup all-purpose flour
1 cup walnuts or pecans, finely chopped

The Cake

2¾ cups all-purpose flour

1 teaspoon baking powder

1 teaspoon baking soda

½ teaspoon salt

1 cup (2 sticks) unsalted butter, softened

¾ cup granulated sugar

½ cup firmly packed light brown sugar

1 tablespoon pure vanilla extract

4 eggs

1 cup buttermilk

1 package (12 ounces) miniature semisweet chocolate pieces

1. Preheat the oven to 350 degrees. Lightly butter a 10-inch tube pan.

2. To make the nut crunch combine the butter, sugar, and flour in a small bowl; stir in the chopped nuts. Spoon the mixture into the bottom and partway up the sides of the prepared pan, pressing in gently. Refrigerate while preparing the batter.

3. To make the cake sift together the flour, baking powder, baking soda, and salt onto a sheet of waxed paper and set aside.

4. In a large bowl, beat the butter, sugars, and vanilla with an electric mixer on high speed until very light and fluffy. Change the mixer speed to medium. Beat in the vanilla, then the eggs, one at a time, beating well after each addition.

continued on next page

Chocolate Chip Cookie Cake (*cont.*)

5. Change the mixer speed to low. Alternately add the flour mixture and buttermilk to the batter, beginning and ending with the flour mixture and beating just until blended. Gently fold in the chocolate pieces with a spatula. Spread the batter in the prepared pan, smoothing the top.

6. Bake until the cake is golden brown on top and shrinks from the sides and tube of the pan, about 70 minutes, loosely covering the top with aluminum foil after 50 minutes if the top is darkening too quickly. Immediately loosen the cake from the pan with a sharp knife, carefully invert onto a wire rack, and turn right-side-up. Scrape out any nut mixture remaining in the pan and pat back onto the cake. Cool the cake completely. Cut carefully with a sharp knife.

Note. If you can't find miniature chocolate pieces, pulse-chop a 12-ounce package of regular-size chocolate pieces or ¾ pound semisweet chocolate in the food processor. The Nut Crunch coating softens up a day or so after the cake is baked, so plan on serving the cake within that time to take advantage of the nice contrast in textures.

Variation. For Mocha Chip Cake, add 2 teaspoons instant espresso coffee powder to the Nut Crunch mixture. Dissolve 2 tablespoons instant espresso coffee powder in 2 tablespoons of hot water; add along with the vanilla to the batter. Increase the baking soda to 1½ teaspoons.

ARABIAN NIGHTS CAKE

This is a cake of whimsy, not too sweet, with Middle Eastern flavors—pistachios, orange flower water, lemon, and cardamom. I like to serve it alongside poached dried fruits and thick yogurt that I buy at my local Middle Eastern delicacy shop. It's also delicious toasted and topped with butter and clear honey. The pistachios can be partially or totally replaced with blanched almonds.

MAKES ONE 10-INCH TUBE CAKE, 12 SERVINGS

1 cup (about 4 ounces) shelled pistachios, preferably unsalted
1⅓ cups sugar plus additional for the top of the baked cake
3 cups all-purpose flour
2 teaspoons baking powder
½ teaspoon salt
1 teaspoon ground cardamom
1 cup heavy or whipping cream
2 teaspoons grated lemon zest
2 tablespoons fresh lemon juice
1 teaspoon pure vanilla extract
2 teaspoons orange flower water
¼ teaspoon almond extract
1 cup (2 sticks) unsalted butter, softened
4 eggs
2 egg yolks
Few drops brandy or rum, for the top of the baked cake

continued on next page

Arabian Nights Cake (*cont.*)

1. Pour boiling water over the pistachios in a heatproof bowl; let stand for 5 minutes, then drain. Working quickly, remove the skins. Let the nuts cool and dry on a paper towel–lined plate, then grind half of the nuts with 2 tablespoons of the sugar in a small food processor or blender and set aside. Chop the remaining pistachios; place on a baking sheet and dry in the oven for 5 to 10 minutes while preheating to 325 degrees; set aside.

2. Generously butter a 10-inch tube pan and set aside.

3. Onto a sheet of waxed paper, sift together the flour, baking powder, salt, and cardamom and set aside. In a 2-cup measure or small bowl, combine the heavy cream, lemon zest and juice, vanilla, orange flower water, and almond extract and set aside; the mixture will thicken.

4. In a large bowl, beat the butter with an electric mixer on high speed until it is light. Gradually beat in the remaining sugar, then the ground pistachios and sugar, and continue beating until very light and fluffy. Change the mixer speed to medium. Beat in the eggs, then the egg yolks, one at a time, beating well after each addition. The mixture may look curdled but this is okay.

5. Change the mixer speed to low. Alternately add the sifted dry ingredients and the cream mixture, beginning and ending with the dry ingredients and beating only until blended. Remove the bowl from the mixer; fold in the chopped pistachios. Spoon the batter into the prepared pan, smoothing the top.

6. Bake until a skewer inserted in the center of the cake comes out clean, about 1 hour. Cool the cake in the pan on a wire rack for 15 minutes. Loosen the cake around the sides and tube of the pan with a sharp knife, then carefully invert onto the rack and turn right-side-up. Sprinkle the cake with a few drops of brandy or rum, then a dusting of sugar. Let cool completely before serving.

HOLIDAY PRESERVES CAKE

Sort of like a fruit cake, but without the preponderance of dried fruit so many people find objectionable. Sour apricot or peach preserves can be substituted for the cherry preserves.

MAKES ONE 10-INCH TUBE CAKE, 20 SERVINGS

2¼ cups all-purpose flour
1¼ teaspoons baking powder
½ teaspoon baking soda
1 teaspoon ground cinnamon
1 teaspoon ground ginger
½ teaspoon salt
1½ cups sugar
1 cup vegetable oil
3 eggs
½ cup buttermilk or plain yogurt
1½ teaspoons pure vanilla extract
1 tablespoon brandy or rum
1½ cups sour cherry preserves (see *Note*)
1 cup walnuts or pecans, chopped
2 tablespoons finely chopped crystallized ginger

1. Preheat the oven to 350 degrees. Generously butter a 10-inch tube pan and set aside. Onto a sheet of waxed paper, sift together the flour, baking powder, baking soda, cinnamon, ginger, and salt; set aside.

2. In a large bowl with the electric mixer on high speed, combine the sugar, oil, and eggs. Change the mixer speed to low. Alternately add the sifted dry ingredients and buttermilk or yogurt, beginning and ending with the dry ingredients and beating only until blended. Beat in the vanilla, brandy or rum, preserves, nuts, and crystallized ginger. Pour the batter into the prepared pan.

3. Bake until the cake shrinks from the sides and tube of the pan and a skewer inserted in the center comes out clean, about 50 minutes to 1 hour. Cool in the pan on a wire rack for 20 minutes. Loosen the cake around the sides and tube, then carefully invert onto the rack and turn right-side-up. Cool completely. Store in a tightly covered container for at least 3 days or up to a week before serving. Or refrigerate for up to 3 weeks.

Note. Sour cherry preserves are tangier than ordinary varieties. If you can't find them, however, substitute regular preserves and reduce the sugar to 1 cup.

CLASSIC SOUR CREAM COFFEE CAKE

No coffee cake book would be complete without one classic sour cream coffee cake recipe. This cake, an adaptation of one created by Jacqui Weeks and given to me by my friend, Grace Kam, is one you'll return to again and again, for Sunday brunches, Christmas mornings, midnight snacks . . . you get the idea! The nuts in the topping toast and the sugar caramelizes, creating a perfect foil for the vanilla-scented cake. Plain yogurt instead of sour cream makes a slightly more tangy cake.

MAKES ONE 10-INCH CAKE, AT LEAST 16 SERVINGS

The Topping
1 cup chopped walnuts or pecans
⅔ cup firmly packed light brown sugar
1 tablespoon ground cinnamon

The Cake
4 cups all-purpose flour
2 teaspoons baking powder
2 teaspoons baking soda
1 teaspoon salt
1 cup (2 sticks) unsalted butter, softened
2 cups sugar
4 eggs

1 pint sour cream or plain yogurt
1 tablespoon pure vanilla extract

1. Preheat the oven to 350 degrees. Generously butter the sides and tube of a 10-inch tube pan and set aside.

2. To make the topping combine the nuts, brown sugar, and cinnamon in a small bowl and set aside.

3. To make the cake sift together the flour, baking powder, baking soda, and salt onto a sheet of waxed paper and set aside.

4. In a large bowl, beat the butter with an electric mixer on high speed until light. Gradually add the sugar and continue beating until very light and fluffy. Change the mixer speed to medium. Beat in the eggs, one at a time, beating well after each addition.

5. Change the mixer speed to low. Alternately beat in the sifted dry ingredients and the sour cream and vanilla, beginning and ending with the dry ingredients and beating just until blended.

6. Spoon half of the batter into the prepared pan and spread evenly. Sprinkle half of the topping over the top. Top with the remaining batter, smoothing even with a spatula. Sprinkle the remaining topping over the top.

7. Bake until the cake shrinks from the sides of the pan, the top is golden, and a skewer inserted halfway between the sides and tube of the pan comes out clean, about 1 hour and 10 minutes. Cool in the pan on a wire rack for 20 minutes, then carefully
continued on next page

Classic Sour Cream Coffee Cake (*cont.*)

invert onto the rack and turn right-side-up. This cake can actually cool completely in the pan.

Variations. For Coconut Sour Cream Coffee Cake, use ½ cup pecans and ½ cup flaked coconut in the topping.

For Raisin Sour Cream Coffee Cake, sprinkle ½ cup regular or golden raisins over the first half of the batter before sprinkling with the first half of the topping.

For Jacqui's Orange-Glazed Coffee Cake, simmer a mixture of ¼ cup frozen orange juice concentrate with ⅓ cup sugar in a small saucepan over moderate heat for 2 minutes; brush the warm glaze over the still-warm cake.

For a smaller coffee cake, halve the batter and topping ingredients. Bake the cake in a 9-inch tube pan for 40 to 50 minutes.

COCONUT TUNNEL OF FUDGE CAKE

This casual cake (owing to the strands of coconut throughout, it doesn't cut very neatly) was inspired by Big Daddy's Cake, a white cake with a chocolate fudge center that appears in Maida Heatter's Book of Great American Desserts. *The mousselike filling is bittersweet; if desired, the unsweetened chocolate can be eliminated for a sweeter taste.*

MAKES ONE 10-INCH TUBE CAKE, 16 SERVINGS

The Chocolate Fudge
1 cup (6 ounces) semisweet chocolate pieces, *or* 2 bars (3 ounces
   each) semisweet or bittersweet chocolate, chopped
1 square (1 ounce) unsweetened chocolate, chopped
3 tablespoons water or coffee
3 tablespoons heavy or whipping cream
2 tablespoons light corn syrup

The Coconut Batter
3 cups all-purpose flour
1½ teaspoons baking powder
½ teaspoon salt
2 teaspoons pure vanilla extract

continued on next page

Coconut Tunnel of Fudge Cake (*cont.*)

¼ teaspoon almond extract
1 cup milk
1¼ cups (2½ sticks) unsalted butter, softened
1⅔ cups sugar
5 eggs
1½ cups (about 5 ounces) firmly packed sweetened flaked coconut

1. Preheat the oven to 350 degrees. Generously butter a 10-inch tube pan and set aside.

2. To make the chocolate fudge combine the chocolate, water, heavy cream, and corn syrup in a small heavy saucepan. Place over moderately low heat and cook, stirring often, until the chocolates melt and the mixture is smooth. Remove from the heat and set aside.

3. To make the coconut batter sift together the flour, baking powder, and salt onto a sheet of waxed paper. Add the vanilla and almond extracts to the milk. Set aside the dry ingredients and the milk.

4. In a large bowl cream the butter with an electric mixer on high speed until light. Gradually add the sugar and continue beating until the mixture is very light and fluffy. Change the mixer speed to medium. Add the eggs, one at a time, beating well after each addition. The mixture may look curdled; do not worry.

5. Change the mixer speed to low. Alternately beat in the sifted dry ingredients and the milk, beginning and ending with the dry ingredients and beating only until combined. Beat in the coconut.

6. Spread the batter in the prepared pan with a spatula, smoothing the top even. Using the bottom of a large spoon, press a trench, about ½ inch deep and 1½ inches wide, around the middle of the top of the batter. Spoon the fudge filling into the trench, avoiding the sides of the pan.

7. Bake until a skewer inserted halfway between the sides and tube of the pan comes out clean, about 1 hour and 20 minutes. Cool in the pan on a wire rack for 30 minutes. Carefully loosen around the sides and tube with a small sharp knife, then invert onto the rack and cool completely.

BOUNTIFUL HONEY CAKE

Honey cakes are synonymous with the holidays in Jewish households. This one, lightly spiced and filled with currants and golden raisins, is topped with walnuts and a baked-on honey glaze. Sturdy, dense, it improves after a day or two. Serve it in wedges or thinly slice it and spread with Orange Cream Cheese (page 226) or Ginger Butter (page 233).

MAKES ONE 9-INCH CAKE, 8 SERVINGS

The Cake
¾ cup honey
½ cup extrastrength coffee
¼ cup firmly packed light brown sugar
⅜ cup (¾ stick) unsalted butter, softened
¼ cup orange juice
1½ cups all-purpose flour
¾ teaspoon baking powder
½ teaspoon baking soda
1 teaspoon ground cinnamon
½ teaspoon ground allspice
½ teaspoon ground ginger
⅛ teaspoon ground cloves
⅛ teaspoon grated or ground nutmeg
¼ teaspoon salt
¼ cup currants

¼ cup golden raisins
2 eggs
¾ cup chopped walnuts

The Honey Butter Glaze
⅛ cup (¼ stick) unsalted butter
¼ cup firmly packed light brown sugar
¼ cup honey

1. Preheat the oven to 350 degrees. Butter a 9-inch cake pan; line the pan with waxed paper, then butter the paper. Set aside.

2. To make the cake combine the honey, coffee, brown sugar, butter, and orange juice in a small saucepan. Bring to a boil over moderate heat, then remove from the heat and set aside.

3. Onto a sheet of waxed paper, sift together the flour, baking powder, baking soda, cinnamon, allspice, ginger, cloves, nutmeg, and salt. Toss 1 tablespoon of the mixture with the currants and raisins; set aside both the dried ingredients and the fruit.

4. In a small bowl beat the eggs with an electric mixer on medium speed until they are well blended. Beat in half of the warm honey mixture until the mixture is smooth, then beat in the remainder.

5. Transfer the sifted dry ingredients back into the sifter and sift again into the honey-egg mixture, a little at a time, mixing in with a wire whip. Mix in the currants and raisins. Spread the batter in the prepared pan. Top with the walnuts.

continued on next page

Bountiful Honey Cake (*cont.*)

6. Bake until the top of the cake is springy and the cake pulls away from the sides of the pan, 45 to 50 minutes.

7. To make the honey-butter glaze, toward the end of the time the cake is baking, combine the butter, sugar, and honey in a small saucepan. Bring to a simmer over moderately low heat, stirring occasionally to dissolve the sugar. Remove from the heat.

8. Pour the hot glaze over the hot cake. Return the cake to the oven. Bake until much of the syrup is absorbed (some will bubble up and remain on the surface), about 5 minutes.

9. Cool the cake in the pan on a wire rack for 15 minutes, then carefully invert the cake onto the rack and turn right-side-up. Cool completely before serving.

POPPY NUT CAKE

More like a Viennese mohnkuchen *than a California-style poppy seed cake, this moist, dense cake is split and sandwiched with raspberry jam for a touch of fruitiness. Because it's layered, it's better as a fork cake than one eaten out of hand. A dollop of* schlag *(whipped cream) with each portion does no harm.*

MAKES ONE 9-INCH CAKE

½ cup poppy seeds
1⅓ cups walnuts
Grated zest of 1 lemon
1 cup all-purpose flour
1 teaspoon baking powder
½ teaspoon ground cinnamon
¼ teaspoon salt
¾ cup (1½ sticks) unsalted butter, softened
1 cup sugar
4 eggs
2 tablespoons dark rum or brandy
1 teaspoon pure vanilla extract

⅓ cup raspberry jam, for spreading between the layers
10× confectioner's sugar, for dusting

1. Preheat the oven to 350 degrees. Butter a 9-inch tube pan and dust with flour, tapping out the excess; set aside.

2. In the workbowl of a food processor, grind the poppy seeds for 3 to 5 minutes to break them up and release their oil. The seeds will darken and become fragrant. Add the walnuts and lemon zest.

continued on next page

Poppy Nut Cake (*cont.*)

Cover and pulse-chop until the walnuts are coarsely ground, then set aside.

3. Onto a sheet of waxed paper, sift together the flour, baking powder, cinnamon, and salt and set aside.

4. In a medium bowl, beat the butter with an electric mixer on high speed until it is light. Gradually add the sugar and continue beating until the mixture is very light and fluffy. Change the mixer speed to medium. Beat in the eggs, one at a time, beating well after each addition, then beat in the rum and vanilla.

5. Change the mixer speed to low. Add the flour mixture, half at a time, then the walnut–poppy seed mixture. Spoon the batter into the prepared pan, smoothing the top.

6. Bake until the cake shrinks from the sides and tube of the pan, the top is springy when lightly pressed with a fingertip, and a skewer inserted into the cake comes out clean, about 50 minutes. Cool in the pan on a wire rack for 10 minutes. Loosen from the pan, then carefully unmold onto the rack and turn right-side-up. Cool completely.

7. To serve, using a sharp knife, slice the cake crosswise in thirds. Place the bottom layer on a plate, then gently spread with half of the jam. Top with the second layer, the remaining jam, then the top layer. Press down gently to adhere. Dust the top of the cake with the confectioner's sugar.

DATE ORANGE CAKE

A very moist, not-too-sweet cake that could be lavished with a cream cheese frosting, if desired; or top with the frosting given in the Variation and decorate with halved dates, walnut halves, and orange slices. Serve with iced orange spice tea.

MAKES ONE 10-INCH TUBE CAKE

The Cake
3 cups all-purpose flour
2 teaspoons baking powder
1 teaspoon baking soda
½ teaspoon salt
1 cup buttermilk
2 teaspoons grated orange zest (from 1 navel orange)
¾ cup fresh orange juice (from about 2 navel oranges)
1 teaspoon pure vanilla extract
1 cup (2 sticks) unsalted butter, softened
1 cup sugar
3 eggs
2 cups walnuts, chopped
1 cup chopped pitted dates

continued on next page

Date Orange Cake (*cont.*)

The Glaze
¼ cup fresh orange juice
¼ cup sugar

1. Preheat the oven to 350 degrees. Butter a 10-inch tube pan and set aside.

2. To make the cake sift together the flour, baking powder, baking soda, and salt onto a sheet of waxed paper and set aside. In a 2-cup measure, combine the buttermilk, orange zest, orange juice, and vanilla and set aside.

3. In a large bowl, beat the butter with an electric mixer on high speed until light. Gradually add the sugar and continue beating until very light and fluffy. Change the mixer speed to medium. Beat in the eggs, one at a time, beating well after each addition.

4. Change the mixer speed to low. Alternately beat in the flour mixture and buttermilk mixture, beginning and ending with the flour mixture and beating just until combined. Beat in the walnuts and dates. Spread the batter in the prepared pan with a spatula, smoothing the top.

5. Bake until the top of the cake is golden, the cake pulls away from the sides and tube of the pan, and a skewer inserted in the cake comes out clean, 1 hour to 1 hour and 10 minutes. Let the cake cool in the pan on a wire rack for 10 minutes.

6. To make the glaze combine the orange juice and sugar in a small saucepan. Bring to a boil over moderate heat, stirring occasionally. Lower the heat and simmer for 3 to 5 minutes, or until the mixture forms a light syrup.

7. Loosen the cake from the pan, carefully invert onto the rack, and turn right-side-up. Place the rack over a piece of waxed paper or aluminum foil to catch any excess glaze, then brush the glaze all over the cake. Let the cake cool completely before serving.

8. The cake improves in flavor and slices more neatly if it is left to rest, loosely covered with aluminum foil, for a day.

Variation. For Frosted Date-Orange Cake, top the glazed cake with the following frosting: Into a medium bowl, sift 2 cups 10× confectioner's sugar. Beat in 1 tablespoon softened butter, 2 tablespoons orange juice, and 1 teaspoon grated orange zest until smooth and of pouring consistency. If the frosting is too stiff to pour, beat in all or part of an additional tablespoon of juice. Decorate the frosted cake with date halves, orange zest strips, and walnut halves.

MAPLE WALNUT STICKY CAKE

This biscuitlike cake pulls apart into 12 individual swirls. It can be kept in one piece and broken up just before serving, or separated and served like sticky buns.

MAKES ONE 9-INCH SQUARE, 12 SERVINGS

¼ cup (½ stick) unsalted butter
½ cup maple syrup
⅓ cup firmly packed light brown sugar
1 tablespoon rum
1 cup walnut halves
2 cups all-purpose flour
1 tablespoon baking powder
½ teaspoon salt
⅓ cup vegetable shortening
¾ cup milk
⅓ cup granulated sugar
1 teaspoon ground cinnamon
2 tablespoons currants or raisins

1. Preheat the oven to 425 degrees.

2. In a small saucepan, melt the butter over low heat. Add the maple syrup, brown sugar, and rum. Continue cooking, stirring just until the sugar dissolves. Remove from the heat and immediately spread the mixture in the bottom of a 9-inch square baking

pan. Sprinkle the walnuts in an even layer over the syrup; set aside.

3. Into a large bowl, sift together the flour, baking powder, and salt. With a pastry blender or 2 knives, cut in the shortening until the mixture forms coarse crumbs. Make a well in the center and pour the milk into the well. Mix with a large spoon just until the mixture forms a dough.

4. Remove the dough to a lightly floured surface. Knead gently 15 to 20 strokes. Do not overknead. Roll out the dough to a 12-by-10-inch rectangle on a lightly floured surface. In a small cup, stir together the sugar and cinnamon and dust over the surface of the dough; scatter the currants over the top. Roll up the dough jelly-roll style, beginning with a long side. Pinch the seam to seal it. Cut, with a sharp knife, into 1-inch-thick slices. (Some of the sugar may fall out.) Place the swirls, cut-sides-down and one right next to the other, in the prepared pan. Tuck the currants into the dough to prevent them from burning.

5. Bake until the tops of the swirls are golden brown and the syrup bubbles up, about 25 to 30 minutes. Let stand 5 to 7 minutes, then carefully loosen the cake from the sides of the pan, invert onto a large plate, and turn right-side-up. Serve warm or room temperature. Carefully scrape any syrup that remains in the pan over the inverted cakes, if necessary.

Note. To plump currants, place in a small saucepan with water to cover. Bring to a simmer over moderate heat. Remove from the heat. Drain thoroughly.

BIENENSTICH

I don't know why there's no honey in this German classic that translates into "Bee Sting Cake." Perhaps the cake, with its baked-on almond topping and custard filling, could lure a bee from its hive?

MAKES ONE 9-INCH CAKE, 8 SERVINGS

The Custard Filling
1 cup milk
¼ cup sugar and pinch salt
2 tablespoons cornstarch
3 egg yolks
1 tablespoon amaretto liqueur
1 teaspoon pure vanilla extract
⅛ teaspoon almond extract
⅓ cup heavy or whipping cream

The Cake
1¾ cups all-purpose flour
2 teaspoons baking powder
¼ teaspoon salt
½ cup (1 stick) unsalted butter, softened
⅔ cup sugar
2 eggs
1 teaspoon pure vanilla extract
¼ teaspoon almond extract
½ cup milk

The Almond Topping
¾ cup blanched sliced or slivered almonds
½ cup sugar
¼ cup (½ stick) unsalted butter, softened
2 tablespoons heavy or whipping cream

10 × confectioner's sugar, for dusting on the baked cake (optional)

1. To make the custard filling combine ⅔ cup of the milk with the sugar and salt in a small heavy saucepan and bring to a boil over moderate heat.

2. Pour the remaining milk into a small bowl; beat in the cornstarch, then the egg yolks.

3. Whisking constantly, add a little of the hot milk to the egg yolk mixture. Bring the remaining milk in the saucepan back to a boil over moderate heat. Whisking constantly, pour the tempered eggs into the saucepan.

4. Cook, whisking constantly, until the mixture comes to a boil. Lower the heat and simmer for 1 minute longer. Immediately remove the saucepan from the heat, stir in the amaretto and vanilla and almond extracts, and pour the custard into a small bowl. Immediately cover the surface of the custard directly with plastic wrap. Refrigerate until cold, up to 24 hours.

5. To make the cake preheat the oven to 350 degrees. Butter a 9-inch springform pan; flour the pan, tapping out the excess, and set aside.

continued on next page

Bienenstich (*cont.*)

6. Onto a sheet of waxed paper, sift together the flour, baking powder, and salt and set aside.

7. In a large bowl, cream the butter with an electric mixer on high speed until light. Gradually add the sugar and continue beating until the mixture is very light and fluffy. Change the mixer speed to medium. Add the eggs, one at a time, beating well after each addition, then beat in the vanilla and almond extracts.

8. Change the mixer speed to low. Alternately beat in the sifted dry ingredients and the milk, beginning and ending with the dry ingredients and beating only until combined. Pour the batter into the prepared pan, smoothing the top even.

9. To make the almond topping combine the almonds, sugar, butter, and cream in a small saucepan and cook over moderate heat until the butter melts. Pour the topping over the cake batter, spreading lightly.

10. Bake until the top of the cake is golden, a skewer inserted in the center comes out clean, and the cake shrinks from the side of the pan, about 40 minutes. Cool the cake in the pan on a wire rack for 20 minutes. Loosen around the sides of the pan with a sharp knife, then carefully remove the pan. Cool the cake completely.

11. To assemble the cake, whip the cream for the custard filling until it forms soft peaks. Stir about 2 tablespoons of the whipped cream into the chilled custard, then fold in the remainder.

12. Slice the cake in half crosswise and place the bottom half, cut-side-up, on a serving platter. Gently spread the custard filling on the cake, then top with the remaining cake layer, cut-side-down. Refrigerate the cake until serving time. Dust lightly with the confectioner's sugar, just before serving, if desired.

CARAMEL ESPRESSO SWIRL CAKE

A rich caramel-macadamia filling swirls throughout this elegant company cake. To intensify the caramel flavor, serve the cake with coffee laced with Liqueur Brûlé. One of my favorites because it is so pretty, this cake keeps moist for several days and is just different enough to garner praise every time I serve it.

MAKES ONE 9-INCH TUBE CAKE, 12 SERVINGS

The Caramel Nut Swirl
½ cup firmly packed light brown sugar (from a 1-pound package; save remainder for cake batter)
¼ cup granulated sugar
⅓ cup heavy or whipping cream
2 tablespoons unsalted butter
2 tablespoons light corn syrup
1 tablespoon instant espresso powder

continued on next page

Caramel Espresso Swirl Cake (*cont.*)

1 cup unsalted macadamias (about 4 ounces), toasted, cooled, and coarsely chopped

½ cup dry cookie crumbs (from 7 Petit Beurre cookies or similar kind)

¼ teaspoon ground cinnamon

The Cake

3 cups all-purpose flour

1½ teaspoons baking powder

½ teaspoon baking soda

¼ teaspoon salt

1 cup sour cream

1 tablespoon instant espresso coffee powder dissolved in 1 teaspoon hot water

1 tablespoon dark rum

1 teaspoon pure vanilla extract

1 cup (2 sticks) unsalted butter, softened

Remaining brown sugar from 1-pound package

3 eggs

2 egg yolks

10× confectioner's sugar (optional)

1. To make the caramel nut swirl combine the sugars, cream, butter, corn syrup, and instant espresso in a 1-quart heavy saucepan. Bring to a boil over moderate heat, stirring occasionally. Reduce

the heat and simmer, stirring occasionally, for 3 minutes. Remove from the heat and stir in the chopped nuts, cookie crumbs, and cinnamon. Let cool. (This can be done ahead, even a day or two before; just be sure to cover and refrigerate until you are ready to bake the cake.) Whether cooled at room temperature or stored in the refrigerator, the caramel mixture will thicken and turn gooey.

2. To make the cake preheat the oven to 350 degrees. Butter a 9-inch tube pan; dust with flour, tapping out the excess, and set aside.

3. Onto a sheet of waxed paper, sift together the flour, baking powder, baking soda, and salt and set aside. In a small bowl, stir together the sour cream, dissolved coffee, rum, and vanilla and set aside.

4. In a large bowl, cream the butter with an electric mixer on high speed until light. Gradually add the brown sugar and continue beating until the mixture is very light and fluffy. Change the mixer speed to medium. Add the eggs and egg yolks, one at a time, beating well after each addition.

5. Change the mixer speed to low. Alternately beat in the sifted dry ingredients and the sour cream mixture, beginning and ending with the dry ingredients and beating only until combined.

6. Spoon half of the batter into the prepared pan, smoothing the top. Top with half of the caramel nut mixture, spooned in a ring 1 inch from the edge and tube of the pan. Top with the remaining batter, smoothing the top.

continued on next page

Caramel Espresso Swirl Cake (*cont.*)

7. Bake for 30 minutes. Spoon dollops of the remaining caramel nut mixture over the cake, again avoiding the edge and tube of the pan. The mixture will start to sink into the cake. Bake until the cake shrinks from the sides and tube of the pan and the top of the cake is golden, about 30 minutes longer. If the cake begins to darken before baked through, loosely cover the top with aluminum foil.

8. Cool the cake in the pan on a wire rack for 30 minutes. Carefully loosen around the edge and tube of the pan, then invert onto the wire rack and turn right-side-up. Cool the cake completely. Dust the top of the cake with sifted 10× confectioner's sugar, if desired, before serving.

CHOCOLATE WALNUT CAKE

This cake is moist enough to be served without its satiny chocolate glaze, but the glaze adds a tailored look and intensified chocolate flavor. Since the recipe makes enough batter for two cakes, it is easier to prepare with a heavy-duty mixer. If desired, the ingredients can be halved to make a single cake.

MAKES TWO 9-INCH TUBE CAKES

The Cakes
1 cup granulated sugar
1½ cups walnuts
4 squares (1 ounce each) unsweetened chocolate
1 bar (3 ounces) semisweet or bittersweet chocolate, *or* 3 squares (1 ounce each) semisweet chocolate
2 cups hot brewed coffee
4 cups all-purpose flour
2 teaspoons baking powder
1 teaspoon baking soda
½ teaspoon salt
1½ cups (3 sticks) unsalted butter, softened
1 package (1 pound) light brown sugar (2⅓ cups)
6 eggs
2 tablespoons bourbon whiskey
1 tablespoon pure vanilla extract
1 cup sour cream

continued on next page

Chocolate Walnut Cake (*cont.*)

The Chocolate Satin Glaze
1 cup heavy or whipping cream
3 bars (3 ounces each) bittersweet or semisweet chocolate,
  chopped, *or* 9 ounces bittersweet chocolate, chopped
1 square (1 ounce) unsweetened chocolate, chopped (optional)
2 tablespoons unsalted butter
2 tablespoons light corn syrup
½ cup chopped toasted walnuts (optional)

1. To make the cakes preheat the oven to 350 degrees. Generously butter 2 9-inch tube pans and set aside.

2. In the workbowl of a food processor, place the granulated sugar and walnuts. Cover and process until the nuts are ground and set aside.

3. In a small heavy saucepan, combine the unsweetened and semi-sweet chocolates with the coffee and cook over low heat until the chocolates melt. Remove from the heat and set aside. Onto a sheet of waxed paper, sift together the flour, baking powder, baking soda, and salt and set aside.

4. In a large bowl, cream the butter with an electric mixer on medium speed until light. Gradually add the brown sugar, then the walnut sugar, and continue beating until the mixture is very light and fluffy. Add the eggs, one at a time, beating well after each addition. Beat in the melted chocolate mixture, bourbon, and vanilla.

5. Change the mixer speed to low. Alternately beat in the sifted dry ingredients and the sour cream, beginning and ending with the dry ingredients and beating only until combined. Divide the batter between the 2 prepared pans.

6. Bake for 50 minutes. Lower the oven temperature to 300 degrees. Continue baking until the cakes are soft and springy on the top and pull away from the sides and tubes of the pans, about 20 minutes longer.

7. Cool in the pans on wire racks for 15 minutes. Carefully loosen around the sides and tubes of the pans, then invert onto the racks and turn right-sides-up. Cool completely before glazing.

8. To make the chocolate satin glaze bring the cream to a boil in a small heavy saucepan over moderate heat. Add the chopped chocolates, butter, and corn syrup, shaking the pan to immerse the chocolate in the hot cream. Let stand for 1 minute, then beat vigorously with a wire whisk. Stir in the chopped walnuts.

9. Place the cakes on wire racks set over aluminum foil to catch any glaze that drips off. Spoon the glaze over the cakes; it will not completely cover them. Scrape the glaze from the foil and re-glaze the cakes. Refrigerate the cakes to firm up the glaze, if desired.

NINA'S ALMOND TORTE

My friend Nina Simon serves this simple, moist cake often, on its own or split and filled with a half cup of melted raspberry preserves. It's also superb served on a pool of Bittersweet Chocolate Sauce with a billowing dollop of Marsala Cream, a combination I enjoyed at the Union Square Restaurant in New York City.

MAKES ONE 8-INCH CAKE, 8 SERVINGS

⅔ cup sugar
½ cup (1 stick) unsalted butter, softened
½ pound almond paste
3 jumbo or 4 extra-large eggs
1 tablespoon kirsch or orange liqueur
¼ teaspoon almond extract
¼ cup all-purpose flour
½ teaspoon baking powder

10× confectioner's sugar, for dusting

Whipped cream or Marsala Cream (page 235) and/or Bittersweet
   Chocolate Sauce (page 236)

1. Preheat the oven to 350 degrees. Generously butter an 8-inch round cake pan; flour the pan, tapping out the excess, and set aside.

2. In a medium bowl, beat together the sugar, butter, and almond paste with an electric mixer on high speed until well blended. Beat in the eggs, liqueur, and almond extract.

3. Change the mixer speed to low. Beat in the flour and baking powder, just until blended. Do not overbeat. Spread the batter in the prepared pan with a spatula, smoothing the top even.

4. Bake until a skewer inserted in the center of the cake comes out clean, 40 to 50 minutes. Let the cake cool completely in the pan on a wire rack.

5. Invert the cake directly onto a platter, turn right-side-up, and just before serving, dust the top lightly with the confectioner's sugar. Serve with whipped cream or Marsala Cream and/or Bittersweet Chocolate Sauce, if desired.

LIGHT AND SPICY
GINGERBREAD

This is inspired by a cake of Swedish origins. Unlike many American versions, it contains no molasses to deepen its flavor.

MAKES ONE 10-INCH TUBE CAKE, 12 SERVINGS

The Cake
¼ cup gingersnap crumbs
1¾ cups all-purpose flour
1 tablespoon ground ginger
2 teaspoons ground cinnamon
1 teaspoon ground cloves
1½ teaspoons baking soda
¾ cup (1½ sticks) unsalted butter, softened
1½ cups firmly packed light brown sugar
¼ teaspoon salt
4 eggs
1 cup sour cream

The Vanilla Glaze
2½ cups 10× confectioner's sugar
6 tablespoons unsalted butter, softened
1 tablespoon pure vanilla extract
2 to 4 tablespoons milk

1. To make the cake preheat the oven to 350 degrees. Generously butter a 10-inch tube pan. Sprinkle as evenly as possible with the gingersnap crumbs and set aside.

2. Onto a sheet of waxed paper, sift together the flour, ginger, cinnamon, cloves, baking soda, and salt and set aside.

3. In a large bowl, cream the butter with an electric mixer on high speed until light. Gradually add the sugar and continue beating until the mixture is very light and fluffy. Change the mixer spread to medium. Add the eggs, one at a time, beating well after each addition.

4. Change the mixer speed to low. Alternately beat in the sifted dry ingredients and the sour cream, beginning and ending with the dry ingredients and beating only until combined. Spread the batter in the prepared pan, smoothing the top even.

5. Bake until a skewer inserted halfway between the sides and tube of the pan comes out clean, about 50 minutes.

6. Cool the cake in the pan on a wire rack for 30 minutes, then carefully invert onto the rack, turn right-side-up, and cool completely.

7. To make the vanilla glaze sift the confectioner's sugar if it is lumpy and combine it in a small bowl with the butter, the vanilla, and enough milk to make a smooth, pourable, but thick glaze. Spoon over the cake. Let stand until the glaze sets.

ONE-BOWL APPLE SPICE CAKE

This cake is the quintessential fall dessert. Serve it with scoops of vanilla ice cream dusted with cinnamon.

MAKES ONE 10-INCH TUBE CAKE, 12 SERVINGS

The Cake
⅔ cup sugar
⅔ cup firmly packed light brown sugar
¾ cup vegetable oil
3 eggs
1 teaspoon pure vanilla extract
2½ cups all-purpose flour
2 teaspoons ground cinnamon
2 teaspoons baking powder
½ teaspoon baking soda
½ teaspoon salt
2 cups finely chopped pared tart apple (Greening or Granny Smith)
1 cup finely chopped walnuts
½ cup raisins

The Cider Glaze
¼ cup granulated sugar
¼ cup firmly packed light brown sugar
½ cup apple cider

¼ cup (½ stick) unsalted butter
¼ cup heavy or whipping cream
Large pinch ground cinnamon

1. To make the cake preheat the oven to 325 degrees. Butter a 10-inch tube pan; flour the pan, tapping out the excess, and set aside.

2. In a large bowl, combine the sugars, oil, eggs, and vanilla. Beat with an electric mixer on medium speed for 2 minutes.

3. Change the mixer speed to low. Gradually sift in 2¼ cups of the flour, the cinnamon, baking powder, baking soda, and salt, mixing just until each addition is absorbed. (The batter will be thick.)

4. Toss the apples with the remaining ¼ cup of flour. Add the apples, walnuts, and raisins to the batter. Spoon the batter into the prepared pan. (It will still be thick.)

5. Bake until a skewer inserted halfway between the sides and tube of the pan comes out clean, about 50 minutes. Cool in the pan on a wire rack for 15 minutes.

6. To make the cider glaze combine the sugars, cider, butter, and cream in a small saucepan. Bring to a boil over moderate heat. Lower the heat and simmer for 5 minutes, or until the sugars are completely dissolved and the glaze has thickened somewhat. Remove from the heat and stir in the cinnamon; let cool 5 minutes.

7. Carefully invert the cake onto the rack set over a piece of aluminum foil to catch the drips and turn right-side-up. Pour the warm glaze over the cake. Cool completely before serving.

ONE-BOWL CARROT CAKE

This extramoist cake needs no embellishment, although it is often topped with a cream cheese frosting. Here, I've given an optional cream cheese glaze.

MAKES ONE 10-INCH TUBE CAKE, 16 SERVINGS

The Cake
3 cups all-purpose flour
1¾ cups sugar
2 teaspoons baking powder
2 teaspoons ground cinnamon
½ teaspoon salt
1¼ cups vegetable oil
3 eggs
1 teaspoon baking soda
⅔ cup buttermilk
1 teaspoon pure vanilla extract
1 can (8 ounces) crushed pineapple in pineapple juice
1 cup chopped pecans or walnuts
½ cup golden raisins
2 cups grated carrots

The Cream Cheese Glaze (optional)
1 package (8 ounces) cream cheese, softened
1½ cups 10× confectioner's sugar, or more as needed

¼ cup fresh orange juice, or more as needed
1 tablespoon grated orange zest (optional)

1. To make the cake preheat the oven to 300 degrees. Generously grease a 10-inch tube pan; flour the pan, tapping out the excess, and set aside.

2. Into a large bowl, sift together the flour, sugar, baking powder, cinnamon, and salt.

3. Add the oil, eggs, baking soda mixed into the buttermilk, and vanilla. Beat with an electric mixer on slow speed until well blended, about 1 minute. Continue beating for 3 minutes longer. The batter will be very thick, almost gluey; do not worry.

4. Stir the pineapple and its juice, nuts, raisins, and carrots into the batter. Pour the batter into the prepared pan.

5. Bake until a skewer inserted halfway between the sides and tube of the pan comes out clean, about 1 hour and 30 minutes.

6. Cool the cake in the pan on a wire rack for 15 minutes. Carefully loosen around the sides and tube of the pan, then invert onto the rack and turn right-side-up. Cool completely.

7. To make the cream cheese glaze beat the cream cheese in a small bowl with an electric mixer on medium speed until it is very light. Gradually beat in the confectioner's sugar, then the orange juice, until the mixture forms a thick glaze. Add more orange juice or sugar, if necessary, to adjust the consistency. Beat in the orange zest. Drizzle the cake with the glaze.

CHAPTER 7

NEW-WAVE COFFEE CAKES

Pineapple "Cheese" Coffee Cake

Low-Fat Banana Tea Bread

Deep-Chocolate Orange Cake

Microwave Triple Gingerbread

California Prune Bread

Pat's Microwave Zucchini Cake

Even though we'd all like to have the time to prepare cakes and eat them at our leisure, reality dictates otherwise. By the same token, not everyone can enjoy butter, eggs, and other rich ingredients with abandon. Enter New-Wave Coffee Cakes, a handful of recipes geared to time and dietary concerns.

Although I'm not an advocate of cross-the-board microwave baking, I've found that some delicious recipes are possible. One recipe, California Prune Bread (page 216), can even be prepared without any special baking pans.

Likewise, lowering the fat and sugar in a cake doesn't have to mean dry, tasteless eating. Happily, reducing the fat also necessitates significantly reducing the sugar; when the batter has less fat in it, the ordinary amount of sugar tastes cloying.

PINEAPPLE "CHEESE" COFFEE CAKE

Nonfat yogurt, drained in cheesecloth for 10 hours, makes a tangy substitute for cream cheese. If you're in a rush, substitute an 8-ounce package of Neufchâtel cheese.

MAKES ONE 9-INCH SQUARE, ABOUT 16 SERVINGS

The "Cheese" Topping
2 cups nonfat plain yogurt
1 egg white
¼ cup plus 1 tablespoon sugar
1 tablespoon all-purpose unbleached flour
½ teaspoon vanilla

The Cake
Vegetable cooking spray
2 tablespoons graham cracker crumbs
1 cup all-purpose unbleached flour
¼ cup sugar
½ teaspoon baking powder
⅛ teaspoon baking soda
Pinch salt

continued on next page

Pineapple "Cheese" Coffee Cake (*cont.*)

1 can (8 ounces) crushed pineapple in pineapple juice
½ cup plain nonfat yogurt
1 egg white
1 teaspoon lemon juice

1. To make the "cheese" topping place the 2 cups of yogurt in a colander lined with 2 layers of cheesecloth; place the colander over a bowl. Refrigerate the yogurt for at least 10 hours, or until most of the whey has drained out of it into the bowl. You should have between ¾ and 1 cup of cream cheese–like yogurt left. (The whey can be used in other baking recipes, if desired, or it can be discarded. This step can be done a day ahead. Place the cheesecloth-wrapped yogurt in a plastic bag and keep it refrigerated until needed.) Combine the yogurt "cheese," egg white, sugar, flour, and vanilla until smooth and set aside.

2. When ready to bake the coffee cake, preheat the oven to 325 degrees. Spray a 9-inch square baking pan with vegetable cooking spray. Sprinkle the interior of the pan with the graham cracker crumbs.

3. To make the cake stir together with a wire whip the flour, sugar, baking powder, baking soda, and salt in a large bowl until well blended.

4. Remove ⅓ cup of pineapple, with as little juice as possible, and set aside. In a small bowl, stir together the remaining pineapple and

pineapple juice, yogurt, egg white, and lemon juice. Add this mixture to the dry ingredients, stirring just until combined.

5. Carefully spread the batter in the pan. Spread the cheese topping over the batter, leaving a ½-inch border all around. Dot the top with the reserved pineapple.

6. Bake until the cake shrinks from the sides of the pan and a skewer inserted in the center comes out clean, about 50 minutes. Cut into squares. Gently remove the squares. Serve warm or at room temperature.

LOW-FAT BANANA TEA BREAD

Cornmeal adds a nutty crunch to this moist, cinnamon-topped loaf. Because of the nonfat yogurt and bananas, the absence of added oil or fat seems irrelevant. What's more, eliminating the fat somehow reduces the need for sugar in the batter, too. Serve slices plain or lightly toasted.

MAKES ONE 9-BY-5-INCH LOAF

The Batter
Vegetable cooking spray
2 cups all-purpose unbleached flour
½ cup cornmeal
½ cup sugar
1 teaspoon baking soda
1 teaspoon baking powder
½ teaspoon salt
4 egg whites
¾ cup plain nonfat yogurt
3 very ripe medium bananas, mashed (about 1½ cups)
1 teaspoon vanilla extract

The Topping
1 tablespoon sugar
½ teaspoon cornmeal
¼ teaspoon cinnamon

1. Preheat the oven to 350 degrees. Spray a nonstick 9-by-5-by 3-inch loaf pan with vegetable cooking spray.

2. To make the batter stir together the flour, cornmeal, sugar, baking soda, baking powder, and salt in a large bowl with a wire whisk until well blended.

3. In a medium bowl, beat together the egg whites, yogurt, mashed bananas, and vanilla until well blended. Pour over the dry ingredients; stir just until combined. Spoon the batter into the pan.

4. To make the topping stir together the sugar, cornmeal, and cinnamon in a cup; sprinkle evenly over the top of the batter.

5. Bake for 40 minutes, or until the loaf shrinks from the sides of the pan and a skewer inserted in the middle comes out clean. Cool in the pan on a wire rack for 10 minutes. Unmold and cool completely before wrapping in a plastic bag. The loaf keeps for a day or two.

DEEP-CHOCOLATE ORANGE CAKE

This is no "chocolate blackout," "death by chocolate," or other indecently choc-olatey concoction. Rather, it's a very moist sponge cake that would be even a bit better with a tiny scoop of vanilla frozen yogurt.

MAKES ONE 10-INCH TUBE CAKE, AT LEAST 15 SERVINGS

Vegetable cooking spray
Dry bread crumbs
2⅓ cups all-purpose unbleached flour
1¼ cups sugar
⅔ cup unsweetened cocoa powder
2 teaspoons baking powder
½ teaspoon baking soda
1 cup plain nonfat yogurt
1 can (17 ounces) apricot halves in heavy syrup
6 egg whites
Pinch salt
Grated zest of 1 small navel orange

1. Preheat the oven to 350 degrees. Spray a 10-inch tube pan with vegetable cooking spray; sprinkle with bread crumbs, tapping out the excess, and set aside.

2. In a very large bowl, combine the flour, ½ cup of the sugar, the cocoa powder, baking powder, and baking soda with a wire whip until well blended. (If any of the dry ingredients are lumpy, sift them instead of just stirring them.)

3. Combine the yogurt and apricot halves and their syrup in the workbowl of a food processor; cover and process until blended, leaving the apricots in tiny chunks rather than completely puréed.

4. In a large bowl, beat the egg whites and the salt until foamy with the electric mixer on high speed. Gradually beat in the remaining ¾ cup sugar in a slow stream. Continue beating until the egg whites form a meringue with stiff, not dry, peaks.

5. Stir the yogurt mixture into the dry ingredients. (The mixture will appear too dry, but don't panic.) Stir in about ¼ of the beaten egg whites, then fold in the remaining egg whites in 2 or 3 additions, adding the orange zest toward the end. Pour the batter into the prepared pan.

6. Bake until the cake begins to shrink from the sides and tube of the pan and the top springs back when lightly pressed with a finger-tip, about 50 minutes. Cool the cake in the pan on a wire rack for 15 minutes. Carefully unmold onto the rack, then turn right-side-up and cool completely.

MICROWAVE TRIPLE GINGERBREAD

Perhaps even more than with regular baking, microwaving quick breads requires precise measuring and timing—there's a little too much batter for the loaf pan, so I microwave ½ cup of the batter in a ramekin. I like to look upon the cupcake, which takes only 1 minute to microwave, as a dividend.

MAKES ONE LOAF AND ONE RAMEKIN, 12 SERVINGS TOTAL

2 cups all-purpose flour
2 teaspoons baking powder
¼ teaspoon baking soda
½ teaspoon salt
2 teaspoons ground ginger
1½ teaspoons ground cinnamon
¼ teaspoon ground cloves
Pinch ground white pepper
¾ cup milk
¾ cup molasses
1 tablespoon minced peeled fresh gingerroot
½ cup (1 stick) unsalted butter, softened
½ cup sugar
2 eggs
½ cup minced crystallized ginger

1. Butter a glass loaf pan and a microwave-safe ramekin; line the bottoms with waxed paper. Onto a sheet of waxed paper, sift together the flour, baking powder, baking soda, salt, ginger, cinnamon, cloves, and pepper; set aside.

2. In a small saucepan, combine the milk, molasses, and gingerroot. Bring almost to a boil over moderate heat, stirring; the molasses should dissolve. Remove the heat.

3. In a medium bowl, beat the butter and the sugar with an electric mixer on high speed until light and fluffy. Change the mixer speed to medium. Beat in the eggs, one at a time, then the sifted dry ingredients. Gradually beat in the hot milk mixture. Stir in the crystallized ginger.

4. Spoon ½ cup of the batter into the ramekin, the remainder into the loaf pan; smooth the tops. Loosely cover with waxed paper.

5. Microwave the ramekin on high power for 1 minute, rotating once. Cool the ramekin directly on a heatproof surface.

6. Microwave the loaf on high power for 7½ minutes, rotating ¼ turn every 2 minutes, and uncovering after 5 minutes. The cake should be springy but not completely baked; it will continue baking as it cools. Cool the loaf directly on a heatproof surface.

7. Carefully loosen and unmold the ramekin and the loaf. They will slice better if allowed to stand a day before serving. Thin slices of the loaf make lovely tea sandwiches when filled with Orange Cream Cheese (page 226).

CALIFORNIA PRUNE BREAD

This cousin of steamed brown bread comes out moist and delicate when prepared in the microwave.

MAKES TWO ROUND LOAVES, 16 SERVINGS

½ cup chopped walnuts
1 jar (16 ounces) cooked prunes in syrup
Grated zest of ½ orange
2 tablespoons orange juice
1 cup all-purpose flour
¾ cup yellow cornmeal
⅓ cup sugar
½ teaspoon baking powder
¼ teaspoon baking soda
⅛ teaspoon grated or ground nutmeg
⅔ cup buttermilk

1. Place the walnuts in a single layer on a paper plate or microwave-safe paper towel. Microwave on high for 2 minutes, stirring once, until the nuts are toasted. Set aside to cool completely.

2. Meanwhile, cut 4 circles of waxed paper to fit the bottom of a 2-cup glass measuring cup. Butter the measuring cup; place 2 of the waxed paper circles in the cup and butter the paper.

3. Drain the prunes, reserving ½ cup of the syrup. Pit and chop the prunes. In a large bowl, combine the prunes and their reserved syrup, orange zest and juice, walnuts, flour, cornmeal, sugar, baking powder, baking soda, nutmeg, and buttermilk until well blended. Spoon half of the batter into the prepared cup. Cover the top of the cup with a piece of microwave-safe plastic wrap, venting in one place.

4. Microwave on medium, rotating the cup halfway through the cooking time, for 6 to 8 minutes, or until a skewer inserted in the center comes out clean. Remove from the microwave; uncover and let stand directly on a heatproof surface for 10 minutes.

5. Carefully loosen the bread from the cup with a knife, then unmold and cool completely.

6. Wash, then butter and line the cup with waxed paper again as in step 2. Repeat the filling and baking process with the remaining half of the batter.

PAT'S MICROWAVE ZUCCHINI CAKE

I often rely on my friend, Pat Baird, author of Quick Harvest, *for microwave specialties. Her zucchini cake, nutty with the addition of whole wheat flour and redolent with spices, is beautifully flecked with green. It really improves with a day's standing, so plan your baking accordingly.*

MAKES ONE 10-INCH FLUTED CAKE, 12 TO 16 SERVINGS

2 tablespoons uncooked oatmeal
1½ cups unbleached all-purpose flour
1 cup whole-wheat flour
1 teaspoon baking powder
1 teaspoon baking soda
1 teaspoon ground cloves
½ teaspoon ground nutmeg
¼ teaspoon ground allspice
¾ cup vegetable oil
¾ cup firmly packed brown sugar
¼ cup granulated sugar
2 eggs, at room temperature
1 cup yogurt or sour cream
2 cups grated zucchini

1. Grease a 10- to 12-cup microwavable bundt pan. Sprinkle with the oatmeal, turning to coat all surfaces well and evenly.

2. In a large mixing bowl, sift together the flours, baking powder, baking soda, cloves, nutmeg, and allspice.

3. In a second large bowl beat together the oil and sugars with the electric mixer on medium speed, until well blended. Add the eggs, mixing until thoroughly combined, stir in the yogurt and the zucchini.

4. Pour the zucchini mixture over the sifted dry ingredients; stir just until blended. Spoon the batter into the prepared pan, smoothing the top even with the back of a spoon.

5. Place the pan in the microwave oven on an inverted microwavable cereal bowl or rack.

6. Microwave on medium for 9 minutes, rotating twice during cooking time. Microwave on high for 5 to 8 minutes, rotating twice during cooking time, or until a toothpick inserted in the center comes out clean. Be careful not to overcook the cake. (It should still be moist on top. When lightly touched with your finger, spots will come off and the cake underneath should be dry.)

7. Let the cake stand on a heat-resistant counter for 12 minutes. Place the cooling rack over the pan, invert, and let the cake cool completely. (Don't be concerned if the top of the cake is very moist and pale. It will dry completely on standing and the color will darken.)

continued on next page

Pat's Microwave Zucchini Cake (*cont.*)

Note. The cake is best when prepared several hours in advance or even the day before serving.

CHAPTER 8

ACCOMPANYING BUTTERS, SPREADS, SAUCES, AND TOPPINGS

Whipped Honey Butter

Ginger Butter

Prune Butter

Marsala Cream

Bittersweet Chocolate Sauce

White Chocolate Nut Spread

Chocolate Mousse Spread

Like a string of pearls on a black dress, a well-chosen topping accessorizes a simple cake or tea loaf, transforming it into something striking. Throughout the book, I've noted my favorite flavor pairings. Undoubtedly, you'll discover your own.

Take advantage of the versatility of the recipes in this chapter. Many of the spreads and butters are great as toast and waffle toppers, too. The sauces pair well with steamed puddings and ice cream coupes.

For teatime, I like to prepare several different toppings to go with a variety of cakes. I've also used some of the spreads as quick fillings for cakes that are cut crosswise into two or three layers and reassembled.

LEMON CURD

In England, this rich and tangy spread is sometimes known as lemon cheese. A cross between a sweet butter and a honey spread, it's delightful served with simple loaf cakes such as gingerbread, honey cake, or date-nut bread. Since the flavor of the lemon predominates, freshly squeezed juice is de rigueur. A few scrapes of lemon zest and/or a splash of lemon-flavored vodka can be added to the just-cooked curd, for more intense flavor.

MAKES ABOUT 1¼ CUPS

1¼ cups freshly squeezed lemon juice
¼ cup (½ stick) unsalted butter
⅔ cup sugar
3 whole eggs
3 egg yolks

1. In a small heavy saucepan, combine the lemon juice, butter, and sugar. Bring to a boil over moderate heat; remove from the heat.

2. In a small bowl, beat together the whole eggs and yolks until they are liquefied. Beating all the time with a heavy wooden spoon, add about ⅓ cup of the hot lemon juice mixture to the eggs, then beat this tempered egg mixture back into the saucepan.

continued on next page

Lemon Curd (*cont.*)

3. Cook over low heat, stirring constantly, just until the mixture thickens, about 1 minute. Remove from the heat; immediately pour into a glass, ceramic, or stainless steel bowl. Let cool to room temperature, then cover the surface directly with a piece of plastic wrap and refrigerate. The curd keeps for 4 days but should not be frozen.

NUTMEG BUTTER

If possible, use freshly grated nutmeg to prepare this simple spread.

MAKES 1 1/4 CUPS

1 cup (2 sticks) unsalted butter, softened
1/4 cup honey
1/2 teaspoon freshly grated nutmeg or more to taste

1. In a small bowl, beat together the butter, honey, and nutmeg until well blended. Cover and refrigerate until serving time. Return to room temperature for easier spreading. The butter keeps for at least one week in the refrigerator.

MAPLE WALNUT BUTTER

If you like a spread with a bit more texture, stir an additional ¼ cup finely chopped walnuts into the blended mixture.

MAKES ABOUT 1 CUP

½ cup walnuts, toasted (see *Note*)
½ cup (1 stick) unsalted butter, softened
⅓ cup maple syrup
¼ teaspoon ground cinnamon

1. Place the walnuts in the workbowl of a food processor; cover and process until the nuts are ground and begin to form a paste.

2. Add the butter, maple syrup, and cinnamon to the food processor. Cover and process until smooth and well blended, stopping the motor and scraping down the sides once or twice.

3. Store the butter in a covered container in the refrigerator. Let come to room temperature before using. The butter keeps for at least one week.

Note. To toast the walnuts, place them in a single layer in a baking pan. Bake in a preheated 300-degree oven until the nuts smell toasted and are golden, usually 15 to 20 minutes. Watch carefully to avoid burning. The nuts continue to toast for a minute or two once they are removed from the oven. Let the nuts cool completely before grinding them.

ORANGE CREAM CHEESE

If you're trying to reduce your fat consumption, substitute Neufchâtel cheese for the cream cheese in this recipe.

MAKES ABOUT 1 CUP

1 package (8 ounces) cream cheese, softened
Pinch salt
⅓ cup 10 × confectioner's sugar
2 tablespoons sweet orange marmalade
1 tablespoon grated orange zest
1 tablespoon orange juice, or as needed

1. In a small bowl, beat the cream cheese with an electric mixer on high speed until it is light and creamy.

2. Beat in the salt, then gradually beat in the sugar. Continue beating until well blended.

3. Beat in the marmalade and orange zest, then the orange juice. Add more orange juice, if necessary, to make the cream cheese softly spreadable.

4. Transfer the cream cheese to a bowl. Cover and refrigerate. Allow the cream cheese to come to room temperature for easy spreading. The cream cheese keeps for several days.

Variation. For Orange-Apricot Cream Cheese, substitute apricot preserves for the orange marmalade.

DUTCH COCOA SPREAD

For Chocolate Truffle Butter, add a tablespoon of Frangelico liqueur to the spread instead of the vanilla extract. For Mexican Cocoa Butter, add ¼ teaspoon ground cinnamon.

MAKES ABOUT 1½ CUPS

¾ cup unsweetened cocoa powder, preferably Dutch process
½ cup hot water
1 cup sugar
Pinch salt
½ cup (1 stick) unsalted butter, cut into pieces
1 teaspoon pure vanilla extract

1. Onto a sheet of waxed paper, sift the cocoa, then transfer the cocoa to the top of a double boiler. Slowly whisk in the water, then the sugar and salt, until the mixture is smooth.

2. Cook over simmering water, whisking constantly, until the sugar dissolves, about 1 minute. Remove from the heat.

3. Whisk in the butter, one bit at a time, beating just until the butter melts and is absorbed. Whisk in the vanilla extract. Let cool completely, then rewhisk to aerate the butter before transferring it to a covered container. Refrigerate for up to one month.

FRESH STRAWBERRY BUTTER

This rosy pink spread is a variation of a recipe that appeared a few years back in Gourmet *magazine. Besides enlivening loaf cakes, it's a natural topper for biscuits and waffles. Cooking the strawberries intensifies their flavor and increases the butter's keeping quality, to up to one week.*

MAKES ABOUT 1¼ CUPS

1 pint strawberries, rinsed, hulled, and halved
¼ cup sugar
2 teaspoons Grand Marnier or other orange liqueur
½ teaspoon grated orange zest
¾ cup (1½ sticks) unsalted butter, softened

1. In the workbowl of a food processor, purée the strawberries. Force the mixture through a fine sieve into a small saucepan. Stir in the sugar.

2. Bring the mixture to a boil over moderate heat. Lower the heat and simmer, stirring occasionally, until the mixture thickens and reduces somewhat, about 10 minutes. Remove from the heat. Stir in the orange liqueur and orange zest. Let cool completely. (This can be done ahead; cover and refrigerate until ready to proceed.)

3. In a small bowl, beat the butter with an electric mixer on high speed until it is light. Gradually beat in the strawberry mixture, a tablespoon at a time, beating well after each addition.

4. Cover and refrigerate the butter until serving time. Allow the butter to return to room temperature for easy spreading.

Variation. For a very quick, though not as vibrant, strawberry butter, mix together equal parts of good-quality strawberry preserves and softened butter, adding a bit of grated lemon and/or orange zest.

CHEESECAKE CREAM

I agree with Richard Sax, the creator of this whipped ricotta cream, which is also a great accompaniment to assorted fresh fruit: If you can get fresh ricotta cheese, the resulting difference in flavor and texture will be marked. The choice of low-fat or full-milk ricotta is yours; even the low-fat variety produces a remarkably rich-tasting result.

MAKES ABOUT 2 CUPS

1 pound ricotta cheese (about 2 cups), preferably fresh
Milk, if needed
⅓ cup sugar, preferably superfine, or to taste
1½ teaspoons pure vanilla extract
Grated zest of 1 small orange (optional)

1. In the workbowl of an electric food processor (do not use a blender for this recipe), place the ricotta cheese. Cover and pulse the machine 2 or 3 times, just until the cheese begins to become somewhat smoother (or place the ricotta in a mixing bowl and beat with a wooden spoon). If the ricotta seems dry and grainy, add a little milk until it is creamy and smooth.

2. Add the sugar, vanilla, and orange zest, blending just until smooth. Transfer the cream to a glass serving bowl. Cover and refrigerate until serving time. The cheesecake cream keeps for two or three days.

VANILLA BROWNED BUTTER

Gently heating butter until it achieves a nut-brown color and flavor adds a whole other dimension to this basic ingredient.

MAKES ABOUT 1 CUP

1 cup (2 sticks) unsalted butter
1 cup 10× confectioner's sugar
½ vanilla bean, *or* 1½ teaspoons pure vanilla extract

1. In a small saucepan over moderate heat, melt the butter; continue cooking until lightly golden, about 7 minutes. Watch carefully to avoid burning.

2. Pour the butter into a medium mixing bowl, leaving behind any darkened sediment in the pan. Cover and refrigerate the butter until it solidifies.

3. Beat the butter with an electric mixer on high speed to aerate it. Slowly beat in the sugar until well blended.

4. Split the vanilla bean and gently scrape the seeds into the butter, or beat in the vanilla extract.

5. Cover the butter and refrigerate until serving time.

Variation. For Browned Pecan Butter, add ½ cup ground pecans to the butter after beating in the sugar.

WHIPPED HONEY BUTTER

With a food processor, this golden spread whips together in a flash. It can also be blended by hand, although the texture won't be as light.

MAKES ABOUT ²/₃ CUP

⅓ cup honey
½ cup (1 stick) cold unsalted butter, cut into 8 pieces

1. Place the honey in the workbowl of a food processor. Cover and process until light, about 1 minute, stopping the motor once to scrape down the sides of the workbowl with a rubber spatula.

2. With the machine running, drop the butter, one piece at a time, through the feed tube. Continue processing until the mixture is smooth and creamy, about 1 minute longer, stopping the motor once to scrape down the sides of the workbowl with a rubber spatula.

3. Store the honey butter, covered, in the refrigerator for up to a week. Return it to room temperature for easy spreading.

Note. To make honey butter by hand, combine the honey and the butter, softened to room temperature, in a medium bowl and whip vigorously with a large heavy spoon until light and creamy.

Variation. For Ginger Honey Butter, add ½ teaspoon each ground cinnamon and ginger and 1 tablespoon minced candied or preserved ginger.

GINGER BUTTER

Ginger's warmth permeates this spread, which is surprisingly good on the Peanut Butter Loaf (page 78).

MAKES ABOUT 1 CUP

½ cup (1 stick) unsalted butter, softened
1 cup sifted 10× confectioner's sugar
1 teaspoon ground ginger
1 tablespoon orange juice
1 tablespoon syrup from preserved ginger or honey
2 tablespoons minced preserved or candied ginger

1. In a small bowl, beat the butter with an electric mixer on high speed until it is creamy. Slowly beat in the confectioner's sugar and ginger, then the orange juice and ginger syrup or honey, and continue beating until the mixture is very light.

2. Beat in the minced preserved or candied ginger.

3. Transfer the ginger butter to a small serving dish. Cover and refrigerate. Allow the butter to return to room temperature before serving, for easy spreading. The butter keeps for at least one week.

PRUNE BUTTER

This intensely flavored spread is great on loaf breads, with or without an accompanying layer of cream cheese. Tightly covered in the refrigerator, it's a good keeper.

MAKES ABOUT 4 CUPS

1 package (12 ounces) pitted prunes
2½ cups freshly squeezed orange juice
1⅔ cups sugar
1 cinnamon stick (optional)

1. In a medium saucepan, combine the prunes, orange juice, sugar, and cinnamon stick, if desired. Bring to a boil over moderate heat. Lower the heat and simmer until the prunes are plump and tender, about 30 minutes.

2. Remove the saucepan from the heat; remove and discard the cinnamon stick. Transfer the prune mixture to the workbowl of a food processor and process until puréed.

3. Return the purée to the saucepan. Continue simmering until the mixture thickens to a spreading consistency, about 20 minutes longer. Cool to room temperature, then spoon into tightly covered containers or jars and refrigerate for up to several weeks.

MARSALA CREAM

This foamy sauce resembles sabayon in texture and flavor, but it can be made almost entirely in advance.

MAKES ABOUT 2 CUPS

2 egg yolks
⅓ cup sugar
1 tablespoon all-purpose flour
¾ cup heavy or whipping cream
Dash salt
¼ cup (½ stick) unsalted butter, cut into pieces and softened
¼ cup Marsala wine

1. In a medium-size heavy saucepan beat the egg yolks with a wire whisk; slowly beat in the sugar and continue beating until the mixture is thick and lemon-colored. Beat in the flour, 2 table-spoons of the cream, and the salt. Refrigerate the remaining cream.

2. Place the saucepan over low heat. Cook, beating constantly with the whisk, and add the butter, bit by bit, until the butter is incor-porated and the sauce thickens, about 10 minutes.

3. Remove the saucepan from the heat and stir in the Marsala. Cover and refrigerate until completely chilled.

4. Close to serving time, beat the remaining cream until it forms soft peaks. Gently fold it into the chilled egg foam.

BITTERSWEET CHOCOLATE SAUCE

Serve with Nina's Almond Torte (page 196), or pour over homemade ice cream sandwiches made from Cream Cheese Pound Cake (page 102) or Florida Coconut Pound Cake (page 104).

MAKES ABOUT 2²/₃ CUPS

½ pound bittersweet or semisweet chocolate, chopped
1 square (1 ounce) unsweetened chocolate, chopped
1 cup heavy or whipping cream
½ cup firmly packed light brown sugar
⅓ cup light corn syrup
¼ cup (½ stick) unsalted butter
1 tablespoon instant espresso powder
Pinch salt
2 tablespoons dark rum
1 teaspoon pure vanilla extract

1. In a small heavy saucepan, combine the chocolates, cream, brown sugar, corn syrup, butter, espresso powder, and salt. Cook over low heat, stirring frequently, until the chocolates melt and the sauce is smooth and thick. Remove the saucepan from the heat.

2. Stir in the rum and the vanilla. Serve warm, or transfer the sauce to a covered container and refrigerate for up to one week.

3. To reheat and liquefy the sauce, spoon it into a heavy saucepan and place over low heat, stirring frequently, until warm. The sauce can also be microwaved on medium power for about 1 minute.

WHITE CHOCOLATE NUT SPREAD

While white chocolate isn't for everyone (and isn't really chocolate at all), I've always enjoyed its sweet sultriness as a change of pace from the other varieties. Although the recipe calls for ground toasted hazelnuts, almonds or pecans would be delicious, too.

MAKES ABOUT ⅔ CUP

1 bar (3 ounces) white chocolate, cut up
½ cup heavy or whipping cream
¼ cup hazelnuts, toasted, skinned, and ground
1 tablespoon cognac

1. Place the chocolate in a small bowl and set aside.

2. In a small heavy saucepan over moderate heat, bring the cream to a boil. Remove from the heat and pour over the chopped chocolate, shaking the bowl to immerse the chocolate.

3. Let stand 1 minute, then beat with a wire whip until smooth. Beat in the ground nuts and cognac, then cover and refrigerate until of spreading consistency, about 1 hour.

CHOCOLATE MOUSSE SPREAD

Swirl this liqueur-boosted sabayon mousse on slices of any plain cake, such as Cream Cheese Pound Cake (page 102) or Very Vanilla Nut Cake (page 106), or use it to cover a whole cake. Any liqueur can be used, although my personal favorites are raspberry and Grand Marnier.

MAKES ABOUT 2 CUPS

2 bars (3 ounces each) bittersweet or semisweet chocolate, chopped, or 1 cup semisweet chocolate pieces
⅛ cup (¼ stick) unsalted butter, cut up, at room temperature
3 egg yolks
3 tablespoons sugar
⅓ cup liqueur such as raspberry liqueur, Grand Marnier, or Frangelico
1 cup heavy or whipping cream
1 tablespoon dark rum

1. In a small heavy saucepan over very low heat, melt the chocolate (or melt the chocolate in the microwave oven for 2 to 3 minutes at medium power). Remove from the heat. Beat in the butter with a heavy spoon, bit by bit, until it melts in. The mixture will be quite thick. Set aside.

2. Put the egg yolks in a heatproof bowl that fits into a saucepan filled with water brought to a simmer without touching the water. With a wire whisk, beat the egg yolks; slowly beat in the sugar, then the liqueur, until the mixture is well blended.

3. Place the bowl over the saucepan. Cook over the simmering water, whisking constantly, until the mixture thickens and increases in volume. Remove from the heat.

4. Beat the hot egg foam with an electric mixer on high speed until the eggs cool completely and become very thick. Stir about ⅓ of the beaten egg mixture into the cooled chocolate; then fold in the remainder.

5. In a medium deep bowl, beat the cream and the rum with an electric mixer on high speed just until it forms soft peaks. Stir about ¼ of the cream into the chocolate mixture; fold in the remainder.

6. Transfer the mixture to a small serving bowl. Cover and refrigerate until set, about 2 hours. The mousse keeps well in the refrigerator for at least four days.

INDEX

INDEX